FARM
(AND OTHER F WORDS)

FARM (AND OTHER F WORDS)

THE RISE AND FALL OF SMALL FAMILY FARMS

SARAH K MOCK

NEW DEGREE PRESS

COPYRIGHT © 2021 SARAH K MOCK

FARM (AND OTHER F WORDS)
The Rise and Fall of Small Family Farms

ISBN   978-1-63676-820-5   *Paperback*

          978-1-63730-222-4   *Kindle Ebook*

          978-1-63730-264-4   *Ebook*

"If you board the wrong train, it is no use running along the corridor in the other direction."

—DIETRICH BONHOEFFER

*For Lila Robbins, who loved farming, for
teaching me how to tell a good story.*

*For Bryan, who loves frisbee, for believing
in this book long after I'd given up.*

*And for the fucking fantastic people whose
financial support brought this book to life.*

May you, too, find the F-words that help you carry on.

CONTENTS

———

INTRODUCTION

———

Standing at the counter with Hannah, we watched a couple and their two small children wander into the shop.

"Anything I can help you with?" Hannah asked, as the adults looked around. Two blue-topped bottles were peeking out of the brown bag swinging at the woman's side.

"We're, uh, just looking," the woman said. The shop was only about ten by twenty feet inside, and was empty but for the counter, a glass-fronted refrigerator, and three white deep freezers. She pried open the nearest one.

"It's all one hundred percent pasture-raised, heritage breed cattle, lamb, and pork, raised organically less than a mile from here," Hannah began, launching into her elevator pitch. The woman nodded vaguely as she listens to how the meat was processed and what cuts are available. She smiled with murmured *thanks* as Hannah ended with, "Let me know if I can recommend something."

The woman reached into the freezer and pulled out a package of paper-wrapped meat, turning to her husband.

"Eight dollars a pound for ground beef, can you believe that?" she said in a carrying whisper. She let the meat clatter back into the freezer and closed the lid with a careless thud.

"Well, thanks," she said, too loudly to be kind, and ushered her family out of the shop.

As they retreated, Hannah deflated, her shoulder slumping.

"You see what I mean?" she said. "It's hard not to be a little grumpy." I was at Hannah's farm-to-table artisanal meats shop about sixty miles from Washington, DC. For a small town, the weekend social scene is lively with urbanites escaping nearby metro areas in search of misty mountain hikes and rustic, wholesome food, and culture experiences. The parking lot beyond the farm store is bustling. A few people came to purchase meat or eggs while I was there, but not many.

"You saw those bottles in their bag?" Hannah continued, venting, "They're from the distillery next door. Those bottles run $100 each. But eight dollars a pound is too much for local, delicious, responsible meat? It's hard to deal with that on the weekends when you've already spent the whole week caring for livestock and running a business." It feels impossible, almost hopeless, she said, when she knows people are comparing her prices to Whole Foods or Walmart.

Banner sales days were few at the store, but for Hannah it was still preferable to the farmers market circuit. That alternative would involve trucking frozen meats to the Washington, DC area in the wee hours of the morning, spending the day in the sweltering heat, and toting most of it back, all for a few hundred dollars' worth of sales on a good day.

"We also tried CSAs [Community Supported Agriculture] and meat drops, but it wasn't worth it with the amount of effort it took to get people involved. We started with one spot in the city for pick up, but people complained they had to go too far, so we had to add a few more locations. We'd publish the dates and times, send them out, send reminders, but people would call mad after missing us and say, 'Well, you didn't send me an email this week' or, 'Can you text me on the day next time?' or, 'Why can't you just bring it to my door?' It was ridiculous. We had to stop doing it for our sanity."

Plus, selling in the city took away one of the reasons Hannah and her husband got into farming in the first place: the community. They opened the farm store hoping to gain a local foothold, and their rural neighbors supported them in some impressive ways. Hannah told me about filing a last-minute application for a national small business contest, and when the farm unexpectedly made it to the semi-final round, she was discouraged by the fact that finalists would be chosen by online voting. She originally thought they didn't have a chance.

"We told some people about it and asked them to vote for us. But we could never have predicted what happened. There's no cell service and not very good internet here, so people—strangers—were literally setting alarms on their phones to remember to vote for us when they got somewhere with service." Despite the low population and lack of connectivity, their neighbors were evangelical, and the farm won the contest and the $50,000 prize. Hannah's eyes went glassy, and her voice was unsteady remembering it.

"We're not even from here," she told me, her voice catching. "We haven't even been here a decade, but people did this amazing thing, and we're so grateful."

The money couldn't have come at a better time. Hannah and her husband had just had a child, and with most of their resources sunk into the farm, cash flow was a constant source of stress. In their nine years on the farm, neither of them had ever pulled a salary. When I met Hannah, they had only recently started breaking even. They achieved that by working eighty to ninety hours a week each, between the farm work, the store, and their off-farm jobs.

"We sunk all of our savings into this," she said, tucking a strand of hair behind her ear purposefully, "We don't have any assets really, since we didn't inherit land, so we're leasing land and paying all the operating costs and doing all the marketing, and trying to raise our son."

"And then people come in here complaining about eight-dollar ground beef," Hannah sighed. By this time, I was awash with righteous indignation, ready to storm after the aforementioned browsers, drag them back into the store, and berate them until they cracked open their wallets. But I was surprised to hear not anger, but sadness, in Hannah's voice. Shouldn't food, she asked, cost enough for farmers to live a decent life?

"Is earning minimum wage too much to expect?" she continued, a faraway look in her eyes, "Shouldn't we still be able to go on a vacation every once in a while, or send our son to college? Right now, farming doesn't allow us to do that. We love it, and we'd love to keep doing it forever. But honestly, I'm not really sure how we could."

A few months after my visit with Hannah, she and her partner decided to shut down the store and the farm and move on. After a decade of pouring their hearts, souls, and sweat into Virginia soil, they picked up and moved to the Northeast, where her husband now works for another farm.

F#!K

Hannah, who requested I not use her name due to ongoing financial issues related to the farm, in many ways exemplifies the ideal of a modern small family farmer. Hannah and her partner are young, well-educated professionals with training in and commitment to ecologically beneficial practices. They are willing and able to make hefty sacrifices and excel at learning on the fly. They understand the importance of selling good food, and even had a caring community and the "good luck" to receive a big chunk of change simply on the inspirational nature of their story. And yet, despite years of effort and investment in their dream, they didn't make it.

How could that happen?

The obvious answer to me in the moment was: it's the consumer's fault. It's the brown bag-toting moms of the world who have the money to pay for better food but simply don't want to. It's the convenience-obsessed city people of DC who couldn't be bothered to meet Hannah halfway. It's communities that won't invest in their own to help keep the people who are trying to feed them afloat.

At the same time, Hannah's story offers a powerful counterpoint to this conclusion. Sure, Hannah's community wasn't showing up every weekend en masse to buy her meats, but they did show up in a big way in another context, one with no direct benefits for them. They mobilized to help the farm win the contest, and not in exchange for meat, but just for the joy of seeing one of their own succeed. At the time, I couldn't reconcile these two seemingly conflicting pieces of information. All I could see was the farm was over, done, gone, and I wanted to know who to blame.

Answering that question is especially important today because we, as a society, desperately want farmers like Hannah to succeed. Not only because her family's story seems to capture something like the American Dream, but because we've decided that farms like Hannah's are our best hope for a future where we eat, and eat well, without destroying the planet. Hannah's farm is what many of us would think of as a "Good Farm"; one that's growing healthy food, led by people going out of their way to do what's best for the environment while striving to be an important part of their community.

We have a lot of ideas about why Good Farms fail, but in general it's chalked up to a failure of the system. This conclusion tracks with our experiences outside of agriculture, where we've become intimately aware of just how deeply many of our systems are failing the people they purport to serve.

The conflicting evidence in Hannah's story was my first indication that our assumptions about *how* the system is failing are incorrect. It seemed to me not only that the system was not serving Hannah, but the strategies which promised to help her fight the system, from "conscious consumerism" to federal and public support for regenerative practices, weren't working either. The people of Hannah's community showed up but weren't willing or able to show up in the way the modern food movement promises they would. It was in digging into the why behind this breakdown in our Good Farm support system that I began to wonder: Who's failing who here? Is it possible that these farms don't serve communities in the way they should—and would that explain the inconsistent support?

At the bottom of this rabbit hole was a question I was shocked to find objectively unanswered. What, exactly, do we mean by a Good Farm?

That's what I aim to figure out in this book—with a combination of anecdotal evidence, hard data, and the suspicion that somewhere there is a flaw in our food systems architecture, so no existing information could be accepted without challenge. Only by understanding what actually makes a farm good, and how to identify one when we see it, can we start to understand how the system is failing the farms we need.

To do this work, we can't take for granted that small family farming is the best form of food production simply because it currently rests on a pedestal. In taking the small family farm out of its privileged station to examine it up close, warts and all, we'll learn why Hannah's farm failed, and how we'll create more resilient farms in the future.

MAKE BELIEVE FARM

Setting aside our bias in favor of small family farms is incredibly difficult. I know because I spent years getting to know farms around the country and the world, looking for evidence that my affection for them was justified. I wanted to prove that small family farms are not only the best form of agriculture, but also an elevated form of existence, one that grows and nurtures the best human traits and curtails the worst. I wanted this to be true because I grew up on a small family farm myself, and I wanted not only to be part of this extraordinary agrarian community but also to prove it was every bit as great as we told ourselves it was.

I'm not alone in this craving. Exposure to agricultural ideals and characters is common in American culture. Old MacDonald's farm came with a catchy jingle, and it taught us farm essentials in our very earliest stages of life. Children's books, TV, games, art, and activities writ large often lean into the primary colors, animals, and simple words of the pastoral setting: a red barn, a green truck, a white sheep, a yellow duck. Very little media for children invites them along to an office, behind the counter at a fast-food restaurant, or down into a mine. In this way, we learn a lot about farms (not *real* farms, mind, but idealized ones) at a very young age, and this helps us internalize that they are safe, nice, gentle places fit for children to learn and grow, because that's what they were for all of us.

Our collective farm-kid-by-proxy upbringing is just the beginning. As adults, farming becomes an expression of patriotism and an intoxicating symbol of Americana embodied in the people who work the nation's land to feed the nation's people. Across the media landscape, we reserve a very special and sacred narrative for farms and farmers.

The simplest version of the agrarian idyll goes something like this: a plucky farmer with a pure heart and dirt under their fingernails falls on hard times, usually because of a manifestation of urban greed. Due to a combination of grit, innovation, blessed-by-the-gods luck, refusal to part with salt-of-the-earth ideals, and community action, the hard time is overcome, the sinners are vanquished, and the farm goes on to flourish.

Sound familiar? This would have been Hannah's story if I had ended it a little sooner. It's also how we tell the story of America itself, as well as the plot of countless books, films, short stories, radio programs, and tall tales. It's familiar, even in its specificity. We know and love this story, and we tell it over and over. That's part of what makes Hannah's story so unsatisfying. The Good Farm, the ultimate underdog, is supposed to triumph.

The tougher pill to swallow is that our "amber waves of grain" love affair with these farms is rooted in hundreds of years of white settler culture. It may seem benign, but the warm, fuzzy feelings we get when we shop at the farmers market or think of Old MacDonald on his farm are irrevocably tied to a version of the American Dream that encouraged white immigrants to take Indigenous land, enslave people to work it, and transform it into cash by whatever means necessary. These are the two faces of America's agrarian dream, and they cannot be separated.

When fantasizing about retiring to a farm one day or fighting to save farms when they seem to be in jeopardy, we may be aiming to serve only the good half of this dream, but in reality, our actions elevate both. The agrarian narrative has a deep psychic hold, not only on farmers, but on all of us, one that intersects our ideas of patriotism, rugged individualism, self-sufficiency, nature, and of course our deep, cultural connection to food.

To interrogate this wholesome small family farm ideal will require more than rational persuasion. It's hard to debate with ideals. For many, myself included, it requires an entire reworking of our mental infrastructure. Not only because our love of small family farms is so pervasive and riddled with complex emotions, but also because this work requires acknowledging that racist atrocities were committed by and on behalf of America's farmers. My Euro-American ancestors, for hundreds of years, believed the end of small family farming justified the means, and to learn that they were wrong and that we have a responsibility to make it right is no simple admission.

WHO IS A FARMER

Throughout the course of this book, you'll meet many farmers. They live all over the country, grow crops large and small, edible and not, valuable and much less so. What you will not find is a cast of farmers split neatly into good farmers and bad farmers. I've gotten the chance to know these people, and I can say with confidence that they are all human beings, united chiefly by their passion, thoughtfulness, pragmatism, and diversity of flaws, chosen because elements of each of their stories illuminate some under-examined piece of the complex puzzle of the American farm system.

Perhaps some of these operators will fit the perception you have of the American farmer, perhaps none will. None of them are perfect, and none of them have all the answers. In the modern food and farm movement (though we are not alone in this), we have an unhealthy affinity for charismatic figureheads. I think it's safe to say that not one farmer discussed in this book is a universal expert whose practices or teachings deserve absolute deference. The thing about the world not being split into good and bad farmers is, it means they're all just people, and no person is beyond critique.

A final note on the farmers you're about to meet, you will find some have requested a degree of anonymity, and I have largely obliged. In an ideal world, all farmers would feel comfortable telling the truth about their work and experiences publicly. In my years working in agriculture, I've learned it is not an ideal world. When a pseudonym is in use, I note it and explain why, but I will say here that in general it is because the US agricultural industry is very small, and those who asked for anonymity expected to face significant personal and/or professional repercussions for publicly discussing their truth. My intention for this book is not to do harm to the people who were brave enough to speak with me. More importantly, no farmer who requested anonymity has an entirely unique experience. Their stories are representative of their sectors, age groups, regions, and markets, and I am confident that the importance of these farmers' experience is not lost by not knowing their exact identity.

In meeting these farmers, I hope you reach the conclusion that the future of American agriculture is not yet decided. A diabolical pair of ideas are out there, on the one hand, that our only hope is to give up on agriculture altogether, and on the other, that the sector's many problems are already righting themselves and we just have to wait out the inevitable shift. Neither idea is true. The future of the American farm system is still unwritten. It can and will be guided and transformed by all its participants.

As we wade into these stories and that uncertain future, you may find battling out deeply engrained agricultural exceptionalism is no easy feat. It is uncomfortable.

One strategy I've found helpful is when you read a sentence you don't like in this book, or one that rubs you wrong way, take a moment to do a brief exercise. Read the sentence again, but replace the words "farm," "farmer," etc. with the "owner/operator," "trade" of your favorite small business (for example, "restauranteur," "restaurant"). Ask yourself if you would feel differently if we were talking about a small, family-owned restaurant or a Main Street shop, doctor's office, or bookstore.

Some farms *are* essential providers of goods and services, but as we've learned anew during the coronavirus pandemic, they don't have a monopoly on that claim. Clean air and water, medicine, food access (through restaurants, grocers, et cetera), shelter, clothing, and healthy human connections are also critical to our existence. If you wouldn't want to provide exceptions to other critical businesses, from whom we expect high-quality, affordable goods and services that don't harm the community in their creation, we must expect farms do the same without exception or excuse.

CHAPTER 1

WHAT THE
ACTUAL FARM

———

America loves farmers, and despite how regularly we are shamed for our collective "agricultural illiteracy," our ignorance has not hindered our national reverence for farmers (Dewey 2017).

Look no further than the Super Bowl, the ultimate competition to win the attention and admiration of America's biggest annual TV audience. In between the game, you'll find, year after year, that farmers and farms appear to connect products with the venerable brand of the American Farmer, the ultimate avatar for rugged individualism, civic-mindedness, compassionate success, and familial affection.

A 2013 Ram Truck commercial, featuring Paul Harvey's broadcast "So God Made A Farmer," is just one example, one which doesn't actually identify or celebrate a specific farmer but instead celebrates the ideal: the American Farmer. God himself made this farmer, Harvey says, because he needed "somebody willing to sit up all night with a newborn colt, and watch it die, then dry his eyes and say, 'Maybe next year.'"

God needed someone "who'd plow deep and straight and not cut corners," someone who could "bale a family together with the soft strong bonds of sharing." In other words, Harvey's American Farmer is a man at the pinnacle of virtue, a truly Good Man. The commercial ends with the text "to the farmer in all of us" making clear "the farmer" here is a euphemism for our best selves (Ram Trucks 2013, 1:58).

In the fog of our immense fond feelings for all things farm-related, it can be easy to forget that no test of virtue is actually involved in becoming a farmer. Though this kind of media might make us feel like all farmers are good people, we know that's not the case. In fact, we've learned in recent years that the very heaven-sent farmers we most cherish are facing a growing threat, namely from the dreaded corporate farms who threaten to evict our sacred agrarians from the land for the sake of profit. A battle has been raging in the countryside for years, we are told, and not very many of our idyllic farms are left. This fact makes it all the more urgent that we, the general public, join the fight alongside American Farmers to protect their Good Farms.

Before we can charge into the breach, however, we first have to figure out how to find the farms we're looking for. This is no simple task. With millions of farms operating across the country, how are we possibly going to know which are the Good Farms among the wicked?

A specific, objective definition of a Good Farm is hard to pin down, but I think many would echo the reasoning Supreme Court Justice Potter Stewart once used: "I know it when I see it" (Lattman 2006).

ANATOMY OF A FARM

A small family farm, in our collective imagination, is a vibrant, multi-species operation located in the picturesque countryside, a few dozen to a few hundred acres in size, with enough space for a quaint farmhouse, a barn and a silo, some grassy pasture, some straight-rowed fields, a pond, and some forest.

Here, noble toil and communion with nature are ways of life. Kids frolic in the hayloft and trout sparkle in the stream. The wood of the kitchen table grandpa made is perfectly aged, the paint peels off the barn door just so, and the farmer's hands always have just the right amount of dirt under the nails. Fresh-baked bread, vegetables straight from the garden, and clothes swaying on the line are commonplace.

This farm doesn't create fabulous wealth, but it supports two adults and their hardy farm kids, and though some years will be lean, the Lord will ensure it all works out in the end. Eventually the kids will go from playing in the hayloft to working there, from running after the tractor to driving it, and the farm will be passed down and live on in the next generation of born-to-be-farmers as their proud parents take their place in the pantheon of farmers passed. This place is a retreat from the chaotic and fast-paced modern world, the setting of a lifestyle that depends on rising early, working hard, and taking pride in the land.

This is a Good Farm. This is the idyllic agrarian setting of our dreams, but also of our experience, of our films, books, art, songs, and poems.

We often elevate and celebrate these Good Farms, and we place them on the forefront of social and political agendas. The published campaign platform of President Joe

Biden rebuked the Trump administration for favoring "large, industrialized farms over small, diversified ones" as well as for "providing loopholes for corporate farms." It goes on to identify the need for the federal government to work directly with "small and mid-sized farmers," to help build their capacity (Biden for President, n.d.). Senator Elizabeth Warren, as a 2020 Democratic primary candidate, also promised to ensure "programs benefit independent family farmers, not the rich and powerful" (Team Warren 2019). Even Senator Bernie Sanders prioritized changing "regulations to improve markets for family farms" (Friends of Bernie Sanders, n.d.).

Vehement, almost religious, support for family farms is not a partisan issue. Former President Donald Trump visited the American Farm Bureau Federation convention three times during his tenure to celebrate family farmers, signing the "Family Farmer Relief Act" in 2019 which made it easier for farms to file for bankruptcy under the special Chapter 12 rules (White House 2019). Throughout his term, Trump gave many speeches like the ones he delivered there, linking family farms, ranches, and other small businesses, and elevating them as "patriots." A simple search of the Trump White House Archival website yields more than seven hundred remarks, proclamations, statements, and releases celebrating American farmers (White House, n.d.).

Beyond political platforms and stump speeches, evidence of our national love of family farms is all around us—in the breathless national headlines raising the alarm about their decline, in popular documentaries on Netflix that make their work visible to the un-agricultural masses, in the dominance of family farms and their likenesses in food and beverage marketing, and in countless works of fiction across the media map.

Unfortunately for our effort to sort through millions of farms, no one is systematically collecting data on the number of kids per hayloft, the rustic-ness of barn doors, or the exact depth of farmers' personal patriotism. Instead, we have only much cruder information with which to find our Good Farms.

The most common, measurable characteristics that offer Good Farm credibility are "small" and "family."

THE FARMLING

A few years ago, I thought I'd found a Good Farm of this very small family persuasion. I met a farmer who checked all the boxes. He was a vital upstart in America's proudest traditions—young, bright, hardworking, a family man with deep agricultural roots, invested in farming practices that preserve the land, and committed to growing healthy food for his community. I set out in the summer of 2017 to meet this dream farmer in his pastoral paradise.

I first met Chris Newman in person in the pre-dawn hours, pulled off a back road in Charlottesville, Virginia. It was chilly for August, but when he jumped out of his pickup, he was wearing a thin white t-shirt. While I shivered and yawned, he crackled with energy.

I had first met Chris months before—online, of all places. I happened upon a blog he'd written about starting a farm after leaving a career as a software executive in Washington, DC. I was struck by his voice, and the fact he was a Black farmer and a member of the Choptico band of Piscataway Indians, starting a farm from scratch in the rural South, so I reached out and asked if we could talk. He invited me along to help with morning chores, and here I was, forcing myself out of my warm car and into the chilly, pre-dawn air.

I followed Chris through a gate and up a steep hill, him talking a mile a minute, me slogging mentally and physically in his wake. The sun had only feebly risen. I empathized. As the world lightened around us, I got a good look at Chris. He was over six feet of wiry frame with just a hint of nerd about him, either because of the springy way he carried himself or the vintage glasses that framed his striking green eyes.

"So this is it mostly," he launched in. "We farm this field, which is about ten acres of pasture and then those woods there," he gestured to the forested edge of the field. "We got involved when we met the woman who owns it. She lives there," he pointed to a mansion about a quarter-mile away. It looked like it had been cut out of an Italian tourism magazine and pasted into this Blue Ridge valley. Meeting and getting to know the landowner had been a particularly lucky break for Chris.

"We don't farm all of it," he added quickly. "She still has another guy; he runs cattle, and he's constantly cutting hay to feed them. I don't understand because you don't need to do that. Look at this place," he swept a long arm along the horizon. At that exact moment, as the sun peaked through the mist and hit the dew-jeweled grass sagging near my shins, the hill positively sparkled. For a moment, I got a taste of the joy and bliss of this experience being part of your job, and I savored it. But then the mist swallowed the sun again, and we continued on.

Chris and his wife Annie had only been farming full-time for a few years. He was inspired after a run-in with Michael Pollan's *The Omnivore's Dilemma*, a lauded 2006 book that helped to launch the slow food movement into the mainstream. A work-stress related health scare gave him the extra push he needed to leave corporate life behind and see if he could make a go at the way of life his ancestors had once lived.

We came upon a circular fenced area at the top of the hill. "Fence" seemed generous, but the chickens inside seemed to respect it. Among the scattered birds was an old-fashion enclosed camper straight out of the 1970s, converted into a rolling chicken coop. These were egg layers, a mix of black and white barred rocks, white leghorns, and fluffy red stars. We checked the feeders and waterers, the hens completely unfazed by our presence.

Beyond the mobile chicken setup, at the edge of the field near the woods, a short electric fence ominously enclosed a seemingly empty pen. As we approached, the *Jurassic Park* vibes escalated.

"Now we only wanted female pigs," Chris explained, stopping alongside the barrier, "and we were very clear with the breeder we only wanted unbred pigs. We weren't looking for piglets." As soon as he'd said it, five, then eight, then twelve smallish, speckled pigs came barreling out of the tall weeds at the far end of the pen, following the sound of Chris's voice.

"And somehow," Chris continued, "we got piglets." This seemed to have caused him equal parts shock, exasperation, and joy, like a pregnant couple finding out about its triplets. Even now, as the seemingly never-ending stream of piglets emerged from the weeds, he looked like he was still overwhelmed to see them, despite the bemused smile on his face. The piglets followed us along the edge of the field, knowing they were about to get breakfast. We fed them in a lean-to with feed purchased from a nearby mill.

We continued to a series of low wire enclosures, each home to about thirty white fluff balls. Chris retrieved and filled plastic waterers from the pens while I studied the flocks of chicks who, far from frightened, seemed only to have a vague interest in our whereabouts. Maybe it was even mild annoyance. These lazy little cotton balls were broiler chickens, just days away from being a pasture-raised addition to someone's table.

After the waterers had been refreshed, Chris explained that each of the pens needed to be dragged about six feet across the field, so a new patch of pasture would be exposed to the pecking, raking, and pooping of the hungry fowl.

The idea that this six-foot by four-foot pen might make its way not only across one acre, but across ten, was mind-boggling. An acre is 43,560 square feet, slightly smaller than a football field. That means this pen could be moved once a day, every day, for just about fifty years in this field before it would find itself occupying the same twenty-four square feet. For context, a big office desk is about six feet by four feet. So when you go to the office, you're working 1/1815ths of an acre.

As we moved the last pen, Chris explained his strategy for the farm. It started with a lot of research, training at a well-known farm in the region, and being well-read in the literature of the slow food and permaculture movements. Much of what he learned complemented his heritage knowledge, and all along he kept his eyes peeled for opportunities to use his engineering skills to improve the status quo. Then the farm became a side hustle; Chris focused on establishing markets, and getting customers, mainly on nights and weekends. His time in tech attuned him to the fact that businesses don't come into the world fully grown; they start small and scale up. He was well-aware that his choice of practices which focused heavily on long-term sustainability, soil health, and animal wellbeing could be costly, but that didn't matter much to him.

He wasn't looking to cash out of his farm, he was looking to build something that lasted in a truly ancient tradition.

Chris had grown up in urban Washington, DC where he planted corn supporting beans and encircled by squash, or three sisters, in his backyard. Chris's father raised his son in the traditions of their Chesapeake Bay tribe, and that history was part of what brought Chris to farming. Yet Chris was not only determined to honor tradition, he wanted to grow healthy and nutritious food while also having a positive impact on the environment. Chris was a student of permaculture methods, of rotational grazing and building closed systems for raising livestock. The holy grail for Chris was the food forest, being able to plant trees, shrubs, and plants that grow harmoniously and yield fruits, vegetables, nuts, even grains.

"That's how Indians use to grow things," he explained. "They didn't just plant their gardens by their houses, they planted them in the sunny patches of the forest floor. I'd love to be able to do that here one day. But I can't be planting trees and making big investments on someone else's land." Without a more permanent land tenure situation, Chris will continue focusing on livestock. He was renting his little slice of farm on an annual basis, and was getting a relatively good deal, due to a combination of good connections and a landlord who bought in on his dream. In a less optimal situation, renting or leasing land can set a farmer back hundreds or thousands of dollars a year per acre (NASS USDA 2020d).

"We've pretty much given up on the idea of buying land," he told me matter-of-factly. I felt a little twinge of sadness at this. Why should owning land be an impossible dream for a new farmer? Part of the challenge is farmland is quite expensive. Among America's most productive soils in Iowa, a single acre will set you back on average about $7,000. In

California, an acre costs nearly $13,000. Here in Virginia, the cost is nearly $5,000 on average (USDA NASS 2020d, 5). But Chris zips by the statement coolly.

We were standing around at this point, kicking the dirt. Chris explained that making money hasn't been easy. He spent almost every moment that he wasn't actively working with animals and keeping up his facilities running around Virginia, selling at farmers markets, pitching his meats and eggs to food truck chefs and restaurants, and thinking up innovative ways to capture more food dollars without jacking up prices. The challenge of making the farm pay was hard enough without trying to own the mud under his boots.

Despite the challenges, Chris genuinely seemed to be well-suited to solving the puzzle that is environmentally responsible farming, an ethic that grows delicious food without impoverishing the farmer. He has experience making businesses more profitable and finding innovative ways to grow companies. Farming presents a novel challenge and unites his connection to his past with his interest in making a tangible difference in the world. If anyone can make it work, I thought, it's this guy. His energy, his curiosity, and his unshakeable commitment to doing things the right way, even when it's hard, felt unstoppable.

Chris's small family farm looks and feels right, according to our Good Farm vision. It's verdant and diverse, teeming with life, though not without its difficulties. His farm's very existence is, quite literally, an uphill battle, but he struggles on courageously, indefatigable in the face of long odds. He remains in our minds and in the minds of his customers vibrant, quaint, and wholesome.

This was four years ago, and Chris doesn't farm in Charlottesville anymore. He is still as unstoppable as he ever was, but he's learned some important lessons since that first farm faded back into the Virginia mists. The farm he was aiming to build back then was an impossible dream.

Despite the ways Chris's farm captured the Good Farm ideal, there was one important aspect where it fell short. Chris learned that no matter how much chicken he sold, no matter how regeneratively he farmed or how many hours he and Annie poured into the business, it was never enough. Expenses continued to pile up. Rent payments, maintenance, basic repairs, and eventually, his customers became weary of his ever-climbing prices. Like Hannah, he wasn't paying himself, he wasn't paying Annie, and he was draining his savings. He simply couldn't make the farm pencil out.

FARMED UP

I wondered how that could be possible when we have such an impassioned, national love for these small family farms. Especially in light of the burgeoning food movement, and the explosion of farmers markets and other avenues where intentional eaters can access and support farmers. If we care so deeply for small family farms like Chris's, how could they possibly fail?

Georgie Smith, a vegetable grower who's been farming in the Pacific Northwest for two decades, told me a story that offered some clarity. Georgie started on Chris's path much earlier, and with access to generational family farmland. She began with a simple vegetable garden, selling her extra produce at her local farmers market. Over time, her dream of a simple, raised-bed garden grew to reclaim the fifteen farmable acres of her family's property. She was planting over two hundred varieties at the operation's peak, in addition to raising pigs and chickens. Georgie knew how to hustle on the marketing end too, but that part of the job didn't seem to be getting easier over time. In fact, it kept getting harder.

"I started with farmers markets, but then the Pacific Northwest got very competitive," she explained to me by phone. "Suddenly, instead of two to three vegetable farmers at the markets, you have like six or seven people with the same stuff." Early on, Georgie said she could make $1,500 at a Seattle-area farmers market in a day. Years later, at the last market she attended, she only made $300.

"The people in the market were walking around saying, 'Your stuff is so beautiful. I'm so excited to see all these farmers here. I just want to support all of you, so let me see. I'll buy your bunch of carrots.' So they'd buy my carrots and then they'd go to the neighbor to buy a bunch of radishes and they'd go the next person to buy lettuce..." What had once been a thirty-dollar sale had become a five-dollar sale. For Georgie, this marked a dissidence between what shoppers at the markets were meaning to do, and what they were actually doing. Buying one bunch of carrots might have made them feel good, but it was not actually providing meaningful support to Georgie's farm or family.

Though the food movement was definitely growing, it hadn't grown enough to accommodate all the new sellers, Georgie realized. She tried selling to grocery stores and restaurants, but those markets were crowded too. Everywhere she turned more and more farmers, new and old, were trying to capture pieces of a pie that weren't really getting any bigger, and her customers were focused on helping as many farmers as possible. Her workload was increasing while her sales dwindled. She was being run ragged. One day, she just realized she couldn't do it anymore. She had to stop.

"That was probably the hardest thing of all because when you're a vegetable farmer, it's all about 'okay, now I'm going to buy the seeds. Let's place the seed order and it's all going to be okay because this year is going to be the year.'" In 2019, she did not place the order. "I sold through the winter and a little into the spring, and when things ran out, that was it."

In all the time I've spent working in agriculture, I'm always struck by how rare it is to hear from farmers who didn't make it. It's like we assume they died when the farm did, as if there's no one to offer insight about how farms decline or what lies beyond the end of a farm. But many of these farmers are still around and understanding their experiences can help us make sense of what's happening on Good Farms like Chris's.

For Georgie, one of the most surprising things about leaving farming was how people reacted to hearing the news.

"So many people say to me, 'Oh, I'm so sad, I'll really miss you at the farmers market, you were my favorite.'" Georgie paused. "I hadn't been to the farmers market for six years. But they still had this vision of me being at farmers markets, and that's who I was, and they wanted to support me."

FARM, INC.

The villain in Georgie's story is, paradoxically, the rise of other farmers. It's an age-old story in economics where high prices and profit lure new entrants into a market, and then increased supply fills the demand, and businesses are forced to lower their prices to compete with the newcomers. But the unusual thing happening here is that price competition is not the key driver at the farmers market. Instead, the problem is the buyers' desire to spread their purchases around. That's the opposite of how consumers usually respond because usually the convenience of a one-stop shop trumps altruism.

Georgie, if anything, should have had a price advantage over newer farmers because they are less well-established, more likely to make mistakes (and thus need to raise their prices to cover their higher costs), and may even have a lower quality product. But another fact of modern farming is that off-farm jobs, done by the farmer themselves or their spouse, often subsidize farm household income. If core family expenses are covered, it's far easier to sell a vegetable or cut of meat for less than it cost to grow it. Doing so will be a net loss for the farm, but net losses are only a problem if the farm is the only source of income for a family. Even then, favorable tax codes can turn even net farm losses into acceptable financial outcomes.

There was no way Georgie could have raised the price of her produce so much that she could make a sale of a bunch of carrots equivalently profitable to a thirty-dollar order. There's no way she could have compelled chefs to pay prices that made her life more livable. Even when sales were booming, Georgie was putting her all into getting seeds in the ground, getting vegetables out, and convincing her community to put it on their table. Even if there had been a clever innovation that could have allowed her business to survive, she didn't have the bandwidth as a solopreneur to seek it.

Georgie's only real option, if she really wanted to stay in business, was to bring in outside capital to get bigger, work harder, capture economies of scale, and find new markets where she could compete against other farm businesses charging at least the cost of production. Competing against those who are not aiming to make a profit is not a viable option for a for-profit business.

Because that's the thing: farms *are* businesses.

We don't tend to think about farms as businesses. In the American mythos, farms exist in a confusing no man's land between business, hobby, lifestyle choice, and religion. This ambiguity is undoubtedly related to the fact that farmers and farm families are considered nearly super-human, intensely more authentic and virtuous, at least, than ordinary people (consider even the connotation of the word "heartland"). In colleges and universities, too, we've exceptionalized Agricultural Business and Agricultural Economics right out of business and economics departments. Instead, they're usually found in agriculture or natural resource departments, a telling illustration that farm businesses are not expected to play by common economic rules.

In truth, the overall data seems to confirm that farm businesses are not widely successful in terms of providing stable income for their owners. Consistently for the last forty years, farm families have, on average, earned less than twenty-five percent of their total income on the farm (USDA ERS, n.d., "Farm Household Income"). In that way, unless these farmers are also taking a vow of poverty, the assumption that scrappy bootstrappers like Georgie and Chris can earn a living and support their family from the land alone does not hold water.

This conclusion seems to justify the agricultural exceptionalism; farmers are not poor through any fault of their own but because of some flaw in the system. Many say farmers deserve exceptions because they continue on in the face of continuous losses for the love of the work.

The problem with this assumption is, at the same time, we live in a world where business failure, however personally sad for those involved, is often a good outcome for the economy overall. Businesses getting out-competed on price, quality, and customer service means conditions for consumers are likely getting better. More farmers at the farmers market means more incentive for them to lower their prices, which means local, fresh food is more accessible to more people.

But as Georgie's story illustrates, her customers weren't discouraged by high prices; more subtle motivations were at play.

HEART(LAND) DISEASE

Naming these motivations reveals an uncomfortable fact of the food movement and our new-found love of farmers markets. When Georgie's customers visited her stall on weekends, their actions show it wasn't about the taste or feel of the produce, the price, or even about Georgie herself. It was about the positive feelings they got from feeling like they're doing their part to support small family farms. That's why their primary goal was to spread their purchases, rather than to find the best deal. It was, in essence, more akin to charitable giving, where the good feelings were magnified by simply transacting with the greatest number of farmers.

That's why customers didn't notice Georgie's six-year absence; because coming to the farmers market was not about building a meaningful relationship with a farmer, or even about acquiring desirable produce, it was about an idea of community that didn't involve anyone in particular. Georgie's product was as much her presence and identity as representative of the Good Farm ideal as was her vegetables.

In that way, those altruistic shoppers at the farmers market aren't Georgie's customers as much as they are benefactors of an agrarian ethos. At best, they provide minimal support to brand new farms through a nascent startup stage. At worst, they were stringing farms like Georgie's along while investing in a farce that makes them feel good and perpetuating farms that likely aren't really viable.

Though both Chris's and Georgie's farms fit our small family ideal, neither were able to survive these economic realities of being a Good Farm.

Put another way, we've been acting for some time now like farming is primarily a moral act when, in fact, it's an economic one. Farming is not a lifestyle. It's a job.

An enormous gap exists between the moral and the economic farmer. The chasm between the soaring ideals of dutiful work, joyful service, soil-grounded patriotism and benevolent people-feeder, and the actual day-to-day struggle of setting up, running, and growing a farm business is impossibly wide and deep. No amount of craving the former can help you successfully do the latter, and a lot of farms die in the pit between what we believe farms should be and what they actually are.

We've heard explanations for why small farms face this particular struggle from farmer-authors and ag-curious journalists for years. Federal farm policy, the modern high-tech, high-input farming practices used by bigger, older, richer competitors, the fact that consumers are uninformed about their food, and the hegemony of Big Grocery and fast food have all been offered as reasons why these small family farms can't make it (Pollan 2006). The solutions offered by these same thinkers are that we should change the world around these farms—change federal policy to favor them, curtail the farming practices of "industrial farmers," forcibly inform consumers, remake fast food with health consciousness in mind, and cut food retailers down to size so these Good Farms can thrive (Bittman et al., 2015).

We should realign the whole system, in other words, and change the diet, preferences, shopping habits, and budgets of consumers at every level of wealth and privilege so small family farms can go on (or "get back to") farming the way they'd prefer. If only we could change everything about the current system, the argument goes, then small family farms would be great again.

This complete overhaul is, obviously, a very tall order. Before we commit to taking on this incredible (and perhaps impossible) challenge, it's worth asking: Do we know for sure that "small" and "family" are the essential ingredients that make a farm good? We assume from those two qualities a lot of other benefits will automatically flow—a focus on community and customer health and access, a deep commitment to environmental stewardship, economic stability, and a livable life for the people involved. But are those reasonable assumptions?

The farms we've seen so far have indeed been committed to community and customer health, but they didn't think they had the freedom to make their products available at prices we'd commonly agree are affordable. They certainly had a commitment to environmental stewardship, but at the cost of their economic stability and the livability of their work. This evidence suggests that the assumed benefits of small family farming are not always natural outgrowths of these farm traits. In fact, it seems some of these benefits might be impossible to achieve within the constraints of the small family farm model.

WILL THE REAL SMALL FAMILY FARM PLEASE STAND UP

If we maintain that small family farms are Good Farms that the overlap in these groups is essentially complete, then in taking a closer look at who is currently claiming the small family farm title (and thus benefitting from our admiration) we should find plenty of farms like Chris's, right?

Let's consider some examples.

Is a square mile covered property line to property line in straight rows of corn or soybean monocultures a small family farm? What about five thousand hogs in a gigantic barn creating enough pig shit to fill something called a manure lagoon? What about rows and rows of almond trees in crumbling gray dirt, sulking in the California desert as far as the eye can see?

Barring additional details, all three of these examples *could* meet the definition of a "small family farm" and would have good reason to seize that socially and politically beneficial title.

The problem is that neither the label "small" nor "family" actually narrows the overall group of American farmers very much. The US Department of Agriculture (USDA) places about 88 percent of US farms in the "small" category (Whitt 2020). By definition, any farm that sells $350,000 a year or less in agricultural products is small (USDA ERS 2021b). Nearly 70 percent of all farms identified by the USDA operate on fewer than 180 acres, which means geographic smallness doesn't narrow it down much either (USDA NASS 2020c). The vast majority of farms are then either geographically small or are small businesses in terms of income, and therefore claim the "small farm" label.

The "family" definition is just as unhelpful in narrowing down the list. According to USDA, a "family farm" is simply a farm in which "the majority of the business is owned by the operator and individuals related to the operator by blood, marriage, or adoption, including relatives who do not live in the operator household." This currently includes around 98 percent of American farms (Whitt 2020). Perhaps it offers some measure of hope to know that if "small family farms" are the victims of a long-term campaign to remove them from the land, the scheme must not be going well.

But this creates a real problem for the small family farm defenders. In our collective imagination, a small family farm looks and acts in very specific, and even uncommon ways. But then how do we square that with the fact that almost all farms can claim the small family farm label?

In fact, because this definition is so broad, it's likely that many of those "large, industrialized" or "corporate farms" that we love to hate identify as "small family farms." And it's likely they benefit as much, if not more, from efforts to support Good Farms as Good Farms do.

In the public's attempt to help a vanishingly small group of our fantastical farms, our efforts are being thwarted at every turn by the fact we don't have a very good way to differentiate the farms we admire most from all the rest. While we might think we know a Good Farm when we see one, it appears the words "small" and "family" are insufficient labels to help us systematically find them.

We need better descriptors by which to identify Good Farms. We need more specific and measurable adjectives that indicate whether farms and farmers are modeling (or at least, attempting to model) all the virtues for which we love them so dearly, and therefore whether they've earned the love, respect, investment, and support we currently heap on essentially all farmers indiscriminately.

So where do we begin our search for more precise defining traits of Good Farms? I think we have to start with a deeper look at the farm narratives we already love.

CHAPTER 2

99 PROBLEMS (AND MONEY IS ALL OF THEM)

———

When I first met Robert, a western rancher wearing pressed jeans and a cowboy hat, the last thing I expected to learn was how much he loves lemons, oranges, and grapefruit. It's not just the fruit. It's the plants that bear them, too.

"I love trees," Robert told me by phone. "I love growing trees. I've been around citrus my entire life. Citrus is dope. It's this amazing evergreen tree; it tastes fucking amazing. It's cultivated all over the world, and probably in places where it's too cold for citrus to grow—that's how much people want citrus. It's amazing, and I love doing it."

These lines capture Robert in a nutshell. Passionate, irreverent, and moved by his work. The problem is Robert is going broke. He hasn't brought home more than $25,000 a year in income in the last decade.

"I'll say our farm was at breakeven up until about 2000," he explains. "Since then, we've been operating at a loss of one form or another and trying to figure out how to make that work." Robert, who asked I not use his last name for fear of reprisal from his industry partners, farms about two hundred acres with his dad a few miles outside a major Southwest metro area. In many respects, Robert appears to run a Good Farm—from its hundred-year history in Robert's family to its focus on food production, from its organic certification to its geographic smallness. Over the past two decades, shifts in the produce industry and reduced access to water have dealt the farm a tough hand, and Robert has seen his costs rise while prices for his citrus remain relatively stagnant. His situation seems dire.

"I've got about as much time as my dad has left alive to figure out how to make this work," Robert told me, and I heard his voice waver. His dad is seventy-five. "If I lose his income stream, I can't continue to farm."

His dad's off-farm income has been the farm's financial backstop, allowing them to continue operating despite hemorrhaging money for the last two decades. Without that cash, Robert guesses, the farm would have been sold and their acres of citrus trees would be uprooted in favor of fancy subdivisions. As the city inches closer, the value of their land continues to rise, turning up the pressure by increasing the tax burden, and making holding out even harder. At the same time, Robert recognizes the ownership of and access to the land for what it is: a high value asset and a personal privilege.

Some real dissidence is present here, which sets Robert's story apart from Chris Newman's. It can be summed up by the farming platitude of being "land rich and cash poor." Robert is flirting with poverty in terms of take-home pay while at the same time immense wealth lies beneath his feet, like having a safe full of gold but no combination to open it. Part of the problem is Robert doesn't own his land personally, and due to a complex and archaic ownership arrangement involving distant relatives, he and his dad are limited in how they can use it. Though even without formal ownership, Robert realizes being able to farm and use the land is still a big advantage most young farmers lack. Plus, he knows he may inherit that ground one day, which puts him in a cohort of heirs alongside some of America's richest people.

ZOMBIE FARMS

In America, we like a poor farmer.

Or maybe it's that we love farmers, and simply believe they are almost universally poor. Our Good Farm vision definitely includes patched-knees, old, rusty pickups, and the infinite utility of bailing twine, all of which fold neatly into the familiar farmhouse aesthetic. Farm poverty comes with a certain holiness. It's the manifestation of the sacrifices necessary to become self-sufficient individuals who put their communities first and themselves second. Maybe this perception is a sign that what makes a farm a Good Farm is not that it's small or family run, but that it's poor.

In the technical sense, "small farm" already means "relatively poor farm." Based on the USDA definitions, the size of a farm is determined by its annual revenue. Given that nearly 90 percent of farms collect relatively small amounts of revenue, it follows that many farms are relatively poor compared to bigger farms. But since a huge range exists between the farms that earn near $350,000 in revenue annually and those that earn nothing, Robert's story is a valuable one for understanding in practice who claims the "poor" farm title, and whether these might be the Good Farms we're looking for.

Confusingly, as we've seen, farmers like Robert are somehow simultaneously rich *and* poor. Despite their deep access to land wealth, Robert and his dad live hand-to-mouth because the income they earn from selling fruit every year just barely covers the costs of producing it. Robert is not the exception, especially among young farmers. If anything, drawing a $25,000 a year salary makes him relatively well-off among peers like Georgie and Chris.

Being caught between vast land wealth and minimal annual farm income is common in American agriculture for many reasons. In the case of Robert's income, he simultaneously suffers from a combination of growing too little food to make the low margin business of wholesaling pencil out and growing too much produce to move it all through more lucrative, direct-to-consumer channels. He doesn't have time or resources to pursue new, better markets. In terms of income, Robert's farm is between a rock and hard place.

Yet somehow, they've managed to keep it suspended there for two decades. So how do they do it?

THE REAL BUSINESS OF FARMING

The agrarian idyll offers one explanation—they do it through sheer grit. But is it possible that those who continue the physically and emotionally painful work of farming in the face of steady losses are truly just motivated by legacy, passion, and duty?

Christine Su says no. She's the founder and former CEO of agtech company PastureMap and has met and worked closely with countless ranchers across the country. She knows this story well and described the underlying issue as farmers and ranchers participating in the McDonald's model. The backstory: a few decades into McDonald's franchise work, an executive took a hard look at the books and famously said, "You're not in the burger business. *You're in the real estate business*" (Haden 2020). Farmers, at least those that own land, are also in the real estate business.

Farmers and ranchers have two separate businesses, Christine explained. The one most often focused on is a farm production business, which in Robert's case is a citrus grove. But the second business is all about real estate. "You're managing land," she told me by phone, "where the strategy is to buy it and hold it as a long-term asset that you may want to develop and monetize one day."

Robert is familiar with these motivations. A lot of people in agriculture, he says, especially older folks, understand the long game they're playing, even if they don't want to admit it.

"Farmland is an investment. All farmers have to do is bide their time. Eventually they'll be able to sell the land, and that will provide for [an] extremely comfortable and privileged life. And their means of accomplishing that is literally just accruing value as time passes." Robert points out that owning farmland in particular helps people pay lower taxes than they would on non-farmland wealth. It also offers good opportunities to pass more wealth to their heirs. "People who want to hold on to generational wealth have found farming a successful way to do that," Robert says.

Much reporting and obsessing about annual farm income misses this fact. As with all businesses, farm owners don't just earn income. Businesses accumulate capital and wealth over time. When a business owner exits, often by selling their business, they get the chance to recoup the investment they weren't necessarily able to pay themselves directly through-out their career. Farm owners benefit tremendously from farmland appreciation, which has been positive in every year since 1990 and which has beat the S&P 500 on returns often in the last fifty years (Elworthy 2020; Nickerson et al., 2012). In that way, owned farmland acts as a store of personal wealth, not unlike an investment account.

What do we do, then, with the argument that farmers like Robert are "land rich and cash poor?" When we look around at the sheer value of farmland, and to the economy beyond agriculture, the answer is evident. Being cash poor, or illiquid, is not a real claim to poverty for a business or a family. Many extremely wealthy individuals and families hold significant assets in relatively illiquid form (we wouldn't call Jeff Bezos "Amazon stock rich, cash poor," for example), and many industries require significant capital to make rel-atively slim margins.

But it seems small farms like Robert's don't make slim margins, they make no margin at all, and it begs the question: How have they managed to stay in business?

NO MONEY, NO PROBLEMS

Each year, many farmers in the US do not make any money off their farms. According to tax filings, the vast majority of farmers may actually be actively losing money farming every year.

To illustrate, consider a year like 2010—a middling year for farm sector income in the last twenty. That year, about 75 percent of sole farm proprietors reported a net loss to the IRS, averaging over -$18,000. Only 19 percent of sole proprietor farmers paid any federal income tax on farm income in 2010

(Williamson 2013). In 2017, a much more challenging year, 75 percent of the IRS-identified two million farmers were still claiming losses, allowing them to collectively avoid thirty billion dollars in taxes (Rosenberg and Stucki 2021a).

In our traditional idea of economics, if a business is actively losing money for long enough (without Silicon Valley-level outside cash infusions) it will eventually go out of business. But for US farmers, many safety features, both public and private, are in place to keep them afloat. In the sink/float metaphor, in fact, you might think of US farms as less of a well-enforced boat and more of a floating bathtub.

One of the most important safety nets perpetuating money-losing small farms is farmland ownership. When a farmer owns their land outright, as long as they can cover basic living expenses and property taxes, they can break even or lose money farming and still maintain good financial health.

This is possible in part due to a farm-specific tax code that provides myriad special exemptions for farm businesses and families. This code allows individuals and companies to write off farm losses, including many family living expenses, when they reside on the farm (DOT IRS 2020). Adding this to the fact that farmland in the US has reliably risen in value for decades and the taxes on those gains are subject to a lower tax rate than any other type of income (USDA ERS 2020b; Tarver 2020), makes owning farmland an attractive place to park wealth, regardless of the farm's year-to-year product sales.

Not to mention that in most states, farms qualify for extraordinarily generous property tax reductions. For example, in New Jersey a mere five acres or $500 in annual sales can relieve a landowner of a good chunk of their property tax burden (Leonard 2019). People like Donald Trump have been able to take advantage of such loopholes. By hosting a goat herd at his Bedminster golf course, Trump dodged about $80,000 worth of property taxes in New Jersey in a single year (Ralph 2018).

The idea of a farm as a tax haven is not a rare or unusual interpretation of farm ownership. In fact, the federal government formally recognizes the use of farm ownership as a tool for creative accountants. As the Farmer's Tax Guide admits, farms whose "principal purpose is the avoidance or evasion of federal income tax" are tax shelters (DOT IRS 2020, 7).

The tax benefits inherent to farming make purchasing a farm a lucrative move for many high-net-worth individuals who don't need to make money farming to make a farm pay. Eligibility for farm tax benefits is not based on how well the farm is run, and in fact when a farm operates at a net loss, owners gain access to write-offs that can relieve their tax burden from earnings beyond the farm (Williamson 2013).

Like Robert, many of us never think of farms as part of a possible tax avoidance strategy because poverty is an assumed aspect of the American Farmer identity, and tax shelters are for the rich, not the poor. In reality, the data indicates only a tiny number of farmers have both low income and low wealth (USDA ERS 2020c). In other words, the vast majority of farmers are not poor at all, neither in terms of income nor wealth. Reflecting on the stories we've heard so far reveals why. A truly poor individual or family would find it nearly impossible to amass the resources necessary to farm; to acquire land, to buy seeds or seed stock, expensive equipment, and other tools. It's not likely poor farmers, in the rare cases they exist, started out that way.

Other programs on the federal, state, and local levels also work to keep farms lucrative, even when farming is not. Federal crop subsidies and insurance instruments tend to get the most attention, but they are just the tip of the iceberg. Lurking beneath are minimal or meekly enforced regulations around environmental and worker protections (Ruhl 2000; Rodman et al. 2016), and conservation programs that allow farmers to receive payments for marginal land they keep out of production (USDA ERS 2019a). A truly complete accounting of public financial support for farmers would also include the billions of dollars invested in research, training, loans, and subsidized insurance provided by the USDA (Lehner and Rosenberg 2019), as well as infrastructure like extensive dam and levee systems that serve little public purpose but to prevent flooding of large swaths of private land (Devine 1995). All of these investments, directly or indirectly, help farms that might have low or negative annual net sales from going under.

Various government systems aren't the only one's infusing a sector riddled with ineffective and unstable farm business ventures. In fact, many never receive any government money at all. The farm I ran as a spunky young farmer fits this description. Yet I benefitted from another form of subsidization, a reasonably limitless and completely forgivable line of credit from the Bank of Dad.

THE MOCK FARM

My dad cites a lot of intangibles these days when he explains why he wanted us kids to grow up on a farm, but one of the most important reasons is that he wanted us to learn about money—about earning, spending, investing, and losing it.

We did this through our 4-H and FFA livestock projects. Each spring, 4-H'ers and FFA members purchase (or birth, if you breed your own) livestock, in our area mostly lambs, piglets, or calves, and raise them to show at the county fair. If you do well, you can sell your show animal at the fair's livestock auction, often for a handsome, well-above-market sum.

4-H welcomes its youngest members at eight years old, and from years eight to eighteen, I and my peers bought, raised, competed with, and sold livestock. For me, the introduction to the business of agriculture was a fascinating puzzle. People eat food, I thought, three times a day. We raise animals and plants, and not just any animals and plants, but award-winning, best-in-show type animals and plants. From what I knew at thirteen about entrepreneurship and investment, I knew if I could just crunch the numbers in the right way, I could figure out how to make a killing.

Every day after school, I poured myself into the work of figuring out how to farm profitably. I read books. I talked to experts. While other kids were updating their MySpace walls, I was dialing up the Internet to check my AOL account for responses to my earnest questions from my local farmer-mentors.

Eventually, I landed on dairy goats. A herd of goats, I reasoned, would be my golden ticket to riches and to endless cuteness and fun. I became an expert in the intricacies of raising goats. I carried around a dog-eared book on the subject for so long in seventh grade I earned the nickname "Goat Girl." I found breeders nearby from whom I could acquire goat kids. I knew exactly what I needed to do and how to do it, but I didn't have the money.

So, I brought my idea to my dad. He was a skeptic. But my pitch was strong, and he agreed that if I wrote up a detailed business plan, he'd consider. I was undeterred. I opened a spreadsheet and started laying out the costs of my grand plan, including fencing and changes to the barn, feeders and feed, milking equipment, the animals themselves, and my labor and occasional help from my dad. The costs were significant (and I was naive enough to leave out costs like electricity, transportation, and rent). Next, I outlined my expected income from milk sales, selling baby goats to other 4-H'ers, and winning prize money at the fair.

Spending outpaced expected income in the first year by a factor of ten. So, I went back to the drawing board. I cut out labor payments first (the love of the work is payment enough, right?). Then I cut out any equipment I could possibly do without. I tweaked my milk prices and production up, but it wasn't enough. I added expected income from other 4-H projects to the bottom line. I added money from my allowance. I raised my hypothetical prices on my hypothetical customers even higher.

In the end, I gave my dad a proposal with a heavy heart. I'd made the numbers work, but I knew they didn't really. Looking back, I realized my dad knew that then, but he made the loan anyway. The now defunct dairy has yet to pay a single dime in interest or principal. In the end, I never even made enough to cover my half of the annual feed bill.

Upon reflection, my mistake was obvious. In choosing goats based on my own interests and preferences, I started from the wrong end of the entrepreneurial equation. A successful business starts with an opportunity, with an unmet need or desire among a customer base who has money to spend on a solution. I should have found my customers first and determined what kind of crop I should raise to meet their needs.

Instead, my preferences and passions drove the endeavor. Maybe for a 4-H kid that's okay because the awards at the county fair are meant to honor passion and hard work. But the food market that I thought would make me rich is much more interested in price, safety, consistency, and convenience. Being passionate about the work is its own reward, not one that is automatically compensated for in the market. Frankly, that made this a hobby farm, not a farm business.

Many will bristle at the idea that any kind of farming is a "hobby" because they believe farming in all its incarnations is too difficult for such a flippant term. But many hobbies are difficult. Skiing, sailing, even painting or running can be physically, mentally, and emotionally engaging, financially costly, and rarely lead to significant profit, at least in part because most people who do these activities aren't expecting one. Most people work another job, or wait until they have significant savings or retirement, to pursue these interests in their spare time. The activity is done out of love even when it doesn't lead to a suitable income. That is, by definition, a hobby.

We know many, perhaps even most, farms in the US are hobby farms, or their other incarnation, retirement farms. How many exactly is hard to say, largely due to imprecise USDA data.

THE SILENCE OF THE FARMS

The problem with the data is that the USDA purposefully casts as wide a net as possible when executing their bi-decadal Census of Agriculture, which is the primary source of hard data on the farm sector in the country. As is often the case when casting a wide net, the Census ends up counting a lot of things that aren't farms. In part because it can be tricky for USDA analysts to tell farms with different goals apart, and in some cases, even to tell the difference between farms and non-farm rural properties.

For example, remember the USDA definition of "small farm" that defines "small" as making less than $350,000 a year? USDA actually separates those farmers into two categories: commercial farms bringing in more than $10,000 a year, and non-commercial farms bringing in less than $10,000 a year (USDA ERS 2021c). Harvard researcher Nathan Rosenberg has harbored suspicions about that non-commercial group for a while, and for good reason. His research has identified 422,225 zero-sales "farms" in the 2017 Census of Agriculture, or about 21 percent of the total number of farms (Rosenberg 2017, 4).

As their name implies, zero-sales farms are simply ones that don't report any sales annually, but that still *could* hit the USDA's minimum threshold to be classified as a farm: $1,000 in annual sales (USDA ERS 2021b). Notably, Nathan told me by email, one or two cows, one hundred acres of grass and woodland "pasture," 1/15th of an acre of berries, or 1/5th of an acre of fruit-bearing trees could each help a property hit that target. Anyone who's ever visited rural America knows many big lawns, open pastures, wetlands, forests, and other land uses in the rural landscape exist. But this lax definition ends up counting many of these rural properties as farms, even when the owners don't intend to make money from farming or don't participate in commercial agricultural activities at all.

Understanding how these non-farms get counted starts with knowing that the Census of Ag, like other such counts, is dependent on survey responses. Survey response rates tend to decrease over time in general surveys, and that effect is likely compounded in agriculture due to the notably private and government-skeptical farmer crowd (USDA NASS 2019c). At the same time, the USDA is motivated to ensure they're counting the maximum number of farms because their reach and resources are ostensibly linked to the number of farms that exist (Koerth 2016).

In areas with low population density but inadequate or no survey responses, the USDA uses a published method to estimate the number of farms that could exist (USDA NASS 2017). This is meant to account for non-responsive farms but may instead be inventing farms that never were or obscuring farms that do, in fact, make sales. In fact, Nathan found, buried in a Census appendix, that 51.2 percent of these zero-sale or near zero-sale farms were added during the adjustment phase, as were nearly 40 percent of all farms "counted" in the 2017 Census of Ag (USDA NASS 2017). In other words, a significant percentage of farms in the Census are not verified but are only estimated or projected to exist, and these assumptions have real consequences.

"Zero-sales farmers," Nathan wrote, "dramatically influenced recent census data on farm income, farm size, and operator age, among other results, due to their substantial share of the overall population." Nathan found almost 40 percent of small farms in the Census "do not participate in any commercial markets for agricultural products, despite USDA data showing that, on average, small farm households have high levels of wealth (even when farm assets are excluded from the total) and low levels of debt" (Rosenberg 2018, 7). In many of these cases, then, zero or even negative farm income likely does not mean these farms are poor, it simply means they're *not* farms. On the contrary, these "poor" farms are more likely the abodes of wealthy ruralites, living the leisurely life of rural gentry.

This information calls into question the reliability of USDA Census of Ag data which is used to ground policymaking throughout the federal government, and which is widely reported in the media. If at least one-fifth of the survey's published data is potentially deeply flawed (and Nathan believes that number could be much higher) due to the fact the farms or farmers they describe are in fact *not* farms or farmers, then it is truly unclear what exactly the overall state of US agriculture, or small family farms in particular, might be.

The problem with turning away from Census of Ag data due to this uncertainty is the presence of few, if any, true alternatives. Despite its fundamental issues, the census data is still the premier information we have on the state of the farm sector. Therefore, I'll use more Census of Ag data throughout this book, but I will not take for granted the USDA figures are to be trusted. I'll point out statistical inconsistencies when we encounter them, and I encourage skepticism of any conclusions reached based on USDA data alone.

Among the zero-sales farms, surely some of the people involved in these operations see themselves as farmers (possibly even "full time" farmers). They might consume all their produce at home or focus on "non-productive" farm activities. Large swaths of the backyard chicken crowd, home gardeners, homesteaders, horse farmers, and many who raise livestock as pets might fit in this category. But it really doesn't matter what a farm produces. If a farm operation reliably breaks even or loses money every year with no workable strategy to change that fact, it's impossible to deny that it is a hobby. These hobby, tax shelter, or investment motivations are paramount for many. Researchers predict as many as two-thirds of the farms counted by the Census of Ag fit one of those categories (Rosenberg and Stucki 2021b).

These farms are not poor. They are paying to pursue an expensive lifestyle and can simply afford to live the way they choose.

All that to say, there's nothing necessarily wrong with hobby farms. Again, I was raised on one. But in light of the myriad tax and federal program benefits farms can receive, it's harder to accept how much public money is backing America's farming habit.

Though government subsidization of farming has been a, if not *the*, core critique of US agriculture for decades, it's clear that the federal government is not the only one actively paying to underwrite the current US farm system. The IRS and state governments, at the very least, are also complicit, and more money still comes from private and even non-profit coffers. The off-farm wealth and income pouring into hobby farms, retirement farms, and farm tax-shelters are also subsidies, backstopping farm businesses that are often first about serving the farmer's wants and needs, not those of the eating public. Given how often governmental subsidization of farming is debated and decried, I hear little broad concern about this private subsidization of the current farm system.

By putting the word hobby in front of a farm, it seems to be benign. But the reality is anything that perpetuates agricultural production despite a long-term failure to see any kind of return simply pays to extend the sector's current problems into the future. The USDA may subsidize America's agricultural status quo in a damaging way, but so do many of the rest of us when we start, support, and fight for these farms. And boy, do we love to fight for farms.

SEND OUT THE FARM SIGNAL

Despite the fact that "saving family farms" often amounts to underwriting private land-wealth with charity, America remains infatuated with the idea. It's not hard to find a narrative in our media landscape about a group of unlikely friends who find a way to save Old Man Jenkins' farm from bankruptcy, whether through historic landmark preservation, identifying an endangered owl or wild horse, raising money, attracting media attention, or potentially just by playing a cinematic prank on the nefarious lawyer who's "doing the deal." This plays out in real life too, and it motivates events like the Farm Aid charity concert, a nearly four-decade old annual festival hosted by Willie Nelson, the whole function of which is to raise money in the name of keeping family farms afloat.

I went to Farm Aid in 2018 where I literally bumped into a farmer whose farm was in dire straits.

After our collision, I managed to make my way into a plastic folding chair across a table from him, shouting an apology over the band warming up in the distance. It was a bright fall afternoon in Burgettestown, Pennsylvania, and we struck up a broken conversation in between percussion and guitar blasts. In the midst of the madness, Donn Teske told me about his farm just north of Manhattan, Kansas. He described his operation, a multi-generation cattle ranch and row crop farm founded in the 1800s.

He told me the expansion of the city of Manhattan had been driving up the value of his land for years, and thus his property taxes (and unspoken: property value). In the face of the third consecutive year of abysmal grain prices and lukewarm beef prices, Donn went to his bank for an operating loan, and they said no. Without operating loans, most farms would need to sell off capital, like farmland, to be able to buy inputs to plant a crop. Being turned down for a loan, in many cases, is the kiss of death.

Donn assumed he was probably going to have to sell the farm in the next couple of years, short of some kind of miracle. It was a shocking story to hear at Farm Aid, a place where Donn was absolutely surrounded by thousands of people who, by their very presence, would seem to indicate their enthusiasm for supporting farmers like him. They were a few hundred feet away, listening to music and sipping craft beers while this farmer sat there, showing me pictures on his phone of his favorite place in the world: the farm he felt incapable of saving.

Talking with Donn was a telling illustration of why and how often our efforts to save farms miss the point. On the one hand, Donn's problems were far too deep and systemic to be addressed by an organization like Farm Aid. Help navigating farm support programs and a few thousand dollars in direct grants, which represent the core of Farm Aid's services for farmers (Farm Aid, n.d.), were not going to be enough to set Donn on a path to profitability. He needed hundreds of thousands of dollars in operating funds just to continue doing what he was doing. Growing something other than commodity grains and beef would take an even greater investment in capital and skills. In other words, a simple hand up, a small cash infusion, or a bit of bridge funding to cover costs is not what was needed to "save" this, or many other, chronically low-income farms.

On the other hand, even the idea of trying to save Donn's farm with charity, in itself, is a bit ludicrous. If the problem is that Donn is getting squeezed by rising property taxes because the value of his land is rising so quickly, a simple solution would be to sell some land to secure the necessary funds to keep farming. Naturally, farmers don't *want* to part with any land, but that the idea the public should come to the aid of farmers who aren't making enough in the market, but don't want to part with any of their considerable wealth, is hard to stomach. Imagine a collector with millions in gold asking for financial support. When asked why they don't sell some gold to meet their needs, the predictable answer is "it all means so much to me, how could I possibly part with it?" Farmland is legacy and heritage, yes, but it's also money, and rarely does anyone want to part with money if they think they can avoid it.

BUT POOR FARMERS FEEL RIGHT

From thirty thousand feet, the poverty of farmers makes sense because we know food is relatively cheap. Consumers in the US spend a lower percent of our income on food than any other country in the world (Plumer 2015). That fact alone seems to validate claims that consumers are to blame for impoverishing farmers. If only prices were higher, it seems, then the Roberts of the countryside could find a way to a comfortable living.

Everything we've learned about the majority of low-income farmers, however, indicates that lack of sales often isn't linked to low prices but is the result of not actively pursuing sales at all. Even for farmers like Robert, who would ostensibly benefit from higher food prices, a modest increase would do little to affect the fundamental economics of his operation, especially compared to the impact such a price hike would have on low-income consumers. The thing is few farmers who grow the food we buy at the grocery store are on the cusp of poverty. They may not offer the small farm vibes we crave, but many commercial farmers who operate at significantly bigger scales than Robert's farm have created profitable businesses and considerable wealth growing and selling food.

According to USDA, even small, relatively "poor" farmers are almost universally wealthier than the average American. In 2019, only two percent of farm households were both in a class of low wealth and low-income. The remaining 98 percent of farm households either had high levels of wealth or high levels of income, and more than 55 percent had both. Those high levels of wealth meant the average farm household had more than one million dollars in assets in 2019, and even median farm household income beat the average American household income by more than $10,000 (USDA ERS 2020c).

Farmers who raise livestock are no exception in terms of wealth, despite the many concerns that have been raised about their plight. Chicken farmers in particular have been highlighted for several years as a group under siege by Big Agribusiness, who leeches away their wealth and leaves farmers powerless and penniless (Last Week Tonight 2015). But researchers have found the median household income for America's small chicken farms is still $69,000 annually, and net wealth for this group is also over one million dollars (Rosenberg and Stucki 2021b).

"The idea that these farmers don't make any money because all they do is farm just isn't borne out," Anne Schechinger told me. She's a senior economics analyst with the Environmental Working Group, a leader in providing transparency on the financial state of American farms. She also noted that even among the poorest farms, only three percent have levels of wealth below the average American household. Other farm "poverty" indicators like bankruptcy rates also don't hold up to scrutiny.

"Bankruptcy rates," she says, "are still so much lower among farms than among small businesses more generally in the US." She points out that the alarmist pronouncements when farm bankruptcy rates climb by a few percentage points usually fail to note when the increase only represents a few hundred bankruptcies out of two million US farms. For example, the farm bankruptcy rate in 2019 rose 20 percent, from around five hundred filings in 2018 to six hundred (Neely 2019). Compared to the failure rate among other small business sectors, the exit rates for both years are miniscule.

THESE ARE NOT THE FARMS YOU'RE LOOKING FOR

Despite all the ways that Robert's farm might look like the embattled Good Farm of our dreams, a deeper examination reveals that the story is more complicated. In truth, while Robert's on-farm income might create the sense and appearance of poverty, the motivation to fund the farm with off-farm income is not simply love of the work. Farming is the method by which to keep hold of vast farmland wealth.

This is true on many of America's millions of low-income farms. The appearance of poverty is used to mask the reality of immense private wealth. In fact, America's 897,400,000 acres of privately held farmland (USDA NASS 2020c, 1), at an average price of $3,160 per acre (USDA NASS 2020d, 4), are worth nearly three trillion dollars. This helps us make sense of the fact that today the average American farmer is a millionaire (USDA ERS 2020c).

If Robert is unable to figure out how to increase his farm's revenue in the next few years, and he gets to a point where they can't cover their property taxes and other expenses, he and his dad may have to sell the farm. If the day comes when Robert has to walk away, he is not without alternatives. He's well-educated and could find a middle-income job outside the sector. Farm business owners, as opposed to farm workers, tend to have much more freedom to choose whether to remain in farming. Few are truly constrained by anything other than a desire to hold land wealth, emotional connections to place, and a desire to do work they're passionate about. This is not the same as the lack of choice and agency inherent in true poverty.

As with any small business, sometimes farms fail, and not always because of an unjust system rigged against them. Sometimes people who want to be farmers aren't cut out to be farm business owners, and that's okay. Sometimes an individual farmer is dealt a bad hand, has a change of heart or circumstance, or in some other way the motivations that made them want to farm in the first place erode, and the farm ends, willingly or unwillingly. This can be heartbreakingly sad, but at its core the death of a farm, like death in general, is not bad. It just is. A farm is an investment with inherent risks, and risks don't always pay off.

Despite all the future uncertainties, Robert doesn't think of himself as poor due to his access to and likely inheritance of farmland.

"Up until the last couple of years," Robert told me bluntly, scoffing a little, "I don't think I ever really considered farming as part of that [wealth] mosaic, and that was dumb and naïve of me." Now that he sees the situation more clearly, it's obvious to him why young farmers have such a hard time acquiring land. If farmland is both a high-value investment vehicle, a lucrative tax shelter, and a desirable hobby, what chance do young agrarians have when they plan to use the land primarily for its least lucrative purpose—actually growing crops? In this way, tenant farmers like Chris and Hannah misunderstand the true smallholder farm model—the key word there being "holder" as in landholder, not farm. Small farmers can sometimes tread water while seeking to buy land, but if they can't afford it, it's only a matter of time before their number is up.

All in all, though the small farm definition would have us believe that most farms are poor, the reality is that vanishingly few are actually poor in the common sense of the word. More to the point, it seems the vast majority would not fit well into our Good Farm fantasy. Paradoxically, many fail to meet our definition by both creating fabulous farmland wealth, and by failing to create enough income to support families. The group of truly poor farmers does not include most farms, but a tiny number, and on a truly poor farm we'd expect farmers to have a significantly reduced ability to pass on the business to the next generation, to steward land, to support their family, and to feed their community. Farming is expensive, and the honestly poor can't sustain it for long.

Poor farms, then, are not universally Good Farms. Eliminating "low-income" as a marker of our dream farms ensures tax shelter farms don't get an automatic pass or assistance, nor do hobby farms or homesteads. It relieves us from the obligation to save every farm business, whether or not it has ever successfully earned income, and in doing so underwriting private wealth with charity. It's okay for us to expect farm entrepreneurs to find their way to financial sustainability, neither consumers nor policymakers are obligated to do it for them.

It's fair to wonder then, if making little or no money isn't a marker of a farm's inherent goodness, maybe making a lot of money is. For now, we'll leave behind the low-income farmers struggling to make their passion pay and visit some farmers in another small wedge of the American farms pie: the rural 1 percent.

CHAPTER 3

FARM THE RICH

———

Clay Govier returned to his family farm in Nebraska in the midst of a corn and soybean boom. Brought on by high demand for a growing corn-based ethanol market and fueled by a massive drought, the golden days of nearly seven dollars a bushel for corn in 2012 (as opposed to the more recent $3.50) made joining the family business a lucrative prospect for many young people.

Today, Clay continues to farm 3,500 acres of mostly corn and soybeans with his father and brother. Since his return, the corn and soybean markets have taken a beating. Checking the prices on the commodity market over the last five years might make you feel bad for Clay. He came to the farm during a peak, and in the years since, farm incomes have declined and the farm economy has been in "crisis."

Reporting about the farm economy over the past five years has gone out of its way to reinforce this image. "'They're Trying to Wipe Us Off the Map.' Small American Farmers Are Nearing Extinction" proclaimed *Time Magazine* (Semuels 2019), "Trade wars, climate change plunge family farms into crisis" decried *CNBC* (Connor 2019), and *The New Yorker* reported "America's Farmers Are in Crisis, and They're

Looking to Trump for Relief" (Sullivan 2018). Judging by these headlines in an already under-reported sector, it's been dire in American farming for years.

Clay's take? "We're doing great."

If prosperity is an indicator of a Good Farm, Clay's farm must be one. The overwhelming amount of higher grossing commercial farmers in the US are farms like his; with a relatively simple commodity-focused crop mix, a small number of employees, significant acreage, and a hefty operating budget. Those last two elements are key; scale is the core of Clay's strategy, and scale in agriculture does not come cheap.

THE BROKEN SLOT MACHINE

So how the heck is Clay weathering this "crisis" so painlessly?

There are many reasons, he says, that things are going well for him. First, there have been some good crop years, like 2018. That year, the harvest was big. The farm sold a lot of grain, but there was a lot of grain on the market, so prices were low. The good news for Clay is due to his participation in Farm Bill risk management programs, the USDA paid the difference between the insured price and the market price of most of his grain. The payout netted the farm at least $74,000 that year, in addition to the income earned selling the crop (EWG Farm Subsidy Database 2021a).

Then there are the bad crop years, like 2019. That year was particularly wet, planting was delayed, crops got flooded out and couldn't be replanted, and there was significantly less crop to harvest come fall. Rather than throwing in the towel and collecting a crop insurance payout, however, Clay pushed ahead, harvesting what he could and selling it at relatively higher prices because of the reduced volume in the market. He still received at least $63,000 in commodity payments, in addition to the income earned selling the crop (EWG Farm Subsidy Database 2021a).

Each year, two different types of subsidized risk management, or insurance-type programs, are available to commodity grain farmers like Clay. The first is what comes to mind when imagining crop insurance—coverage that protects farmers against having to swallow the full impact of bad weather or other catastrophes. Farmers pay a subsidized rate for this insurance product, the cost of which is dependent on multiple factors and can range wildly in different regions. According to Clay, he can purchase crop insurance for about $15–$20 an acre for corn, and if the crop is damaged or completely wiped out, he will be compensated up to 75 percent of what he would have received for an average crop at the market price.

The other type of risk management, the one that paid out over $130,000 to Clay's farm between 2018 and 2019, is not crop insurance but a Farm Bill program that farmers simply sign up for rather than paying to participate. These programs, called the Agricultural Risk Coverage (ARC) and Price Loss Coverage (PLC), are meant to support farm revenue (USDA FSA 2019, 2). These are complex programs, but in essence they are direct payments that are meant to grow during "hard times" and get smaller (though notably, not disappear) during "good times." For example, ARC-County, a subset of ARC programs, sends a payment to farmers when revenues across their whole county fall below a historical benchmark. A farmer who elects PLC, on the other hand, will be paid the difference between the market price and a Farm Bill-determined benchmark price for a certain number of bushels (2–4).

Considered separately, both of these programs make sense, especially for lawmakers who, in the past at least, were trying to protect the incomes of the huge part of the US population that once lived on farms. It hasn't been too hard a sell, even now that less than one percent of Americans farm, due to the common narrative that farmers are poor and consistent victims of "unfair" market and weather forces.

Considered together, however, these programs go well beyond ensuring farmers don't go broke due to catastrophic events. Instead, farmers usually receive payments every year because they're protected against bad weather *and* low prices. One of these two is almost always occurring because bad weather leads to good prices, and good weather (and thus high production) leads to low prices. Combined, these programs look less like insurance, and a lot more like guaranteed annual income for farmers out of taxpayer pockets. In the words of one agricultural economist I spoke to, these programs are essentially just money-dispensers and "nobody complains about a broken slot machine that keeps paying out."

Today's farmers are overwhelmingly wealthier and earn higher household incomes on average than non-farm households (USDA ERS 2020c). Guaranteeing income for this group seems problematic at best and even more of an issue is the fact that the nature of the programs themselves encourage farmers to grow a very narrow list of commodity grains. Therefore, farmers like Clay are incentivized, year after year, to keep as many acres as possible in his highest yielding and high payment crops: corn and soybeans.

ZERO FARMS GIVEN

"Crop insurance lets farmers push the easy button," Clay told me admonishingly, "apply excessive amounts of fertilizer, do some recreational tillage, spray your herbicides and insecticides, and then just grow corn on corn on corn, forever." He says these programs enable and even reward bad management practices, and fail to encourage farmers to rotate crops, diversify their operations, and respond to consumer demands. To him, this makes them a terrific waste of taxpayer money.

"No farmer would be farming the way they do right now if it wasn't for the Farm Bill because it would be way too risky," he said. Many farmers, he added, don't even see it as an entitlement payment (which it is, by the US Senate's official definition). They see it as a critical part of their business; something they can't live without.

Federal payments don't end there, either. Every year since 1995, Clay's farm has also received conservation payments. These are "earned" by implementing conservation practices as defined by the USDA, which might include everything from planting cover crops to preserving native plants around waterways to simply removing land from production. Annually, these payments might only account for a few thousand dollars, but Clay says in some years he earns tens of thousands, as conservation grants and cost-shares can also be used for projects like setting up greenhouses or installing irrigation and field drainage tile.

On top of all these benefits, since 2018 farms like Clay's have also had access to Market Facilitation Payments (MFP). The USDA made these "trade aid" payments to compensate farmers for the losses caused by the trade war with

China triggered by Trump administration policies. MFP checks were in addition to risk management payments and accounted for tens of billions of dollars between 2018 and 2020 (CRS 2019). By the end of 2020, because of an additional direct payment package called the Coronavirus Food Assistance Program, more than $96 billion in direct payments were made to farmers over the course of the Trump administration (USDA ERS 2021d). Around $46 billion were sent directly to farmers in 2020 alone (Charles 2020).

Though many of these payments were ad hoc, others were created by the Farm Bill, which has been rewritten every five years since 1933. The most common justification offered for this legislation is the need to invest in American food security. The argument goes that farms must be subsidized because if they were not, the carnage that free market conditions might inflict would fundamentally undermine the nation's ability to feed itself (Farm Bureau, n.d.).

However, most of these payments go to support the production of commodity grains, the overwhelming leaders being corn and soybeans. Commodity corn is not your familiar sweet corn; it's harvested dry and hard and largely used for animal feed, corn ethanol production, industrial applications (it's commonly used in plastics), or refined into sweeteners or other food additives (NCGA, n.d.). Commodity soybeans are often planted in rotation with corn, and more than 50 percent of all soybeans planted in the US are exported, mainly for animal feed (USDA ERS 2021e). Food-grade corn and soybeans, which are used to make corn flour and soy products, from tofu to protein powder, are grown in such tiny quantities compared to their industrial-grade competitors that they're essentially a rounding error.

This news will not come as a surprise to many who believe "corporate agriculture" is diverting the resources small farmers need to survive. The truth is USDA programs were *never* set up to serve small farms. As far back as the early 1900s, implementing the "modernist blueprint" for American agriculture, as Pete Daniel writes in *Dispossession*, "required not only trimming away sharecroppers, tenants, and small owners but also providing subsidies and tax advantages for larger farmers to invest in machines and chemicals…by World War II, the USDA bureaucracy had become a silo that primarily fed substantial farmers" (Daniel 2013, 9). For at least a century, the unstated goal of US farm policy has been to support big farms, cheap food, and keep as many workers in the nonfarm workforce as possible.

This evidence suggests vast redistribution of taxpayer dollars to wealthy farmers is not a perversion of the system, it's exactly the way the system is supposed to function. The problem isn't that the federal farm system is broken. The problem, for small farms at least, is that it works.

We know these commodity farms largely don't grow food for people, but the amount of support they've accumulated suggests what they grow must still be important. So what, exactly, is a commodity crop? To understand America's highest income farmers, we have to understand commodity farming.

THE FARMERS' MARKET

One of the most common adages in agriculture comes from then-Senator John F. Kennedy's 1958 speech, when he said farmers "pay retail, sell wholesale, and pay the freight both ways" (John F. Kennedy Presidential Library and Museum, n.d.). The reality behind this idea has shifted, but that middle part of this equation—the "selling wholesale" part—is largely due to the fact that most commercial farmers sell commodity crops.

An overwhelming amount of total cropland in America is planted in commodity corn, soybeans, wheat, and cotton. Three-quarters of all US farmland is devoted to the commodity production of either grains, oilseeds (like soybeans), or cattle for meat or dairy (USDA NASS 2019b). Almost any agricultural crop, from apples to zucchini, can be and often are sold as a commodity.

What makes these products commodities? Essentially, a commodity is any product that is so uniform and consistent that individual units are indistinguishable, despite coming from different sellers. Commodities aren't unique to agriculture; oil, coal, gold, and many other raw inputs are often sold at a near-universal per unit price for a standard quality, or a commodity price.

Commoditization in agriculture was formalized more recently than you might expect, and the overall benefits have been significant, especially for farmers. Without formal commodity markets, running a business that depends on selling or purchasing an agricultural product, be it cotton for textiles or corn to make whiskey, becomes difficult and expensive.

Consider a baker in Chicago in 1897, just prior to the establishment of the US's first formal agricultural commodity market. They need wheat to make bread, and they need it to arrive by a certain time. Their best bet is to go straight to the farmer, but to make this deal happen in a pre-commodity market world the baker, as a wheat buyer, would have to track down a wheat grower, evaluate the wheat they have for sale (or will have for sale in the future), and negotiate a price. A wheat farmer would have to do this process in reverse, spending significant time marketing, negotiating, selling, and then delivering the grain. Each one of those steps can be costly, time intensive, and introduces risk for both baker and farmer. A formal commodity marketplace bridges this gap between buyer and seller by standardizing price, quality, and the location where transactions take place.

Today, when American farmers reference the commodity market, they are likely thinking of the Chicago Board of Exchange (CME). The CME was established to provide a central market for commodity trading, and in doing so, reduced the costs for all parties involved in these processes. Doing so helped level the playing field for independent farmers and other small businesses that were, in the absence of a formal market, much more likely to be at the mercy of bigger, more knowledgeable, and better-resourced competitors.

To accomplish this field-leveling, formal commodity markets first set specific standards for products. Though these standards were, at one point, set, evaluated, and enforced by the exchange itself, common commodity standards are now enforced by the USDA as part of the Grain Inspection, Packers, and Stockyards Administration. Wheat standards, for example, define exactly how much foreign material a bushel of wheat must contain and how much of it can be damaged and in what ways (USDA GIPSA FGIS 2014).

In creating a standard around a uniform and consistent product, commodity markets reduce the cost of marketing and discovery. There's no need for a baker to compare quality or price between many farmers in the commodity market. Instead, they can be confident they're purchasing a standard product at a known price.

The commodity exchange also acts as a physical locale, a version of a farmers market where buyers and sellers can assemble in one location to wheel and deal. In this setting, a common price is established and continuously updated. These prices are based on supply and demand, and because of the vast number of sellers and the relatively large number of buyers, markets for commodities are particularly competitive. Economically, that means that across the whole sector, absent any shocks (like a drought or a big change in demand), the commodity price will tend to hover around the average cost of production. In other words, whoever grows their commodity most cheaply can set the lowest price, which will help them win the sale even if it's mere pennies above their break-even costs.

In modern agriculture, commodity markets are usually perceived as constraining to farmers, if not as outright failing them. This is in part because when prices are equal to the average cost of production, many farmers will just break even, a few will profit, and many will endure net losses. This driving down of prices in competitive markets, many economists would argue, is good for consumers, but for many farmers it feels like forcing them to sell at an unsustainable price.

The problem is this is how markets in a capitalist system are supposed to work. Free markets work best when they're highly competitive, with many buyers and many sellers bidding the price to where resources are distributed in the most optimal way. Low prices are supposed to be the mechanism that weeds unproductive farmers out of the market. Commodity prices being "too damn low" is yet another piece of evidence, not that the system is broken, but that it's working as it's meant to.

Low commodity prices for decades have been the bane of the farm economy. Even when they're high, it's often only a temporary "boom" cycle that will inevitably crash into a bust. So then why do farmers continue to grow and sell commodity crops?

For one, it allows farmers to focus on what they prefer, like driving the tractor and planting seeds, rather than spending time building markets, serving customers, and handling logistics. To sell into the commodity market, most farmers just need to truck their grains into the nearest town and sell it to the grain elevator (the local grain-aggregating middleman) for the commodity price on the spot, minus some possible fees—no muss, no fuss. Plus, when paired with federal farm programs, growing commodity grain is incredibly low risk for all the reasons we've discussed.

Of all the possible crop options, commodity grains are also one of the least demanding in terms of labor. Centuries of farm technology has been developed and perfected to make this kind of farming maximally productive with minimal work. From the very genetics of plants to chemicals and from implements to software, everything about the commodity grain world has been fine-tuned for uniformity and predictability. Clay's 3,500 farmed acres, five-and-a-half square miles, provides enough work for only three full-time farmer-owners and one part-time worker. In short, commodity grain farming, done conservatively, tends to be relatively reliable, lucrative, and easy.

This extends right down to the annual calendar. Outside of a few busy windows, farmers might be spending some time in the office doing administrative work or scouting fields for issues, but there's also plenty of time to get away for multiday conferences in both the summer, to fly to Washington, DC and lobby Congress, and even to become a snowbird when Nebraska winters start to chafe. Not to mention many farmers find they can operate even a relatively large number of acres of commodity grains on nights and weekends around another full-time job.

GIG FARMER

That is not to say a commodity grain grower never goes out of business. Take Lyle Benjamin, a wheat and small grains grower from Montana. After growing up on a fifth-generation farm, he got the opportunity to farm a more complex, 2,000-acre farm nearby.

To accommodate those acres and keep his landlords happy, Lyle needed to upgrade equipment to the tune of about a million dollars, in addition to costly annual purchases of chemical fertilizer and pesticides.

"The timing of that equipment purchase was a little awkward," he told me by phone, "because I bought it in 2012, which was essentially the peak of all the grain markets," which also means it was the peak of farm machinery prices. As commodity prices plummeted, so did the value of his new implements, until he was underwater. Then a multi-year drought hit, leaving him with low yields, high input costs, debt, and rent to pay. I asked him about the final straw, the thing that made him realize he needed to get out.

"The last year I farmed, 2019, my income was a third from crop production, a third from crop insurance, and a third from government subsidy programs," he said, "I looked at that and I said, 'Man, if only a third of my income is coming from what I'm actually doing, how sustainable is this...?' And I ultimately decided it wasn't." So, Lyle pulled the plug and walked away. He works as an agronomist now in the area, though he misses driving the tractor.

Lyle's situation is different from Clay's because he was renting land, not being a landowner himself. When a farmer has to cover not only all the expenses of operating a farm in a highly competitive commodity sector, but also the costs of competitive land rents, there is much less room for error. Farmers like Lyle who rent all their land and own none, so-called tenant farmers, are rare today, accounting for just 7 percent of total farms (USDA NASS 2019b). Though nearly 40 percent of all farmland in the US is rented, most is rented by large farmers who operate it in addition to their owned acres (USDA NASS 2019b).

Between full farmland ownership and tenancy exists farmers who are still paying off their farmland. This group is often portrayed as being in a particularly vulnerable financial position, similar to renters. Indeed, real estate debt including mortgages on purchased farmland is the biggest source of debt on US farm balance sheets (USDA ERS 2021a). Managing debt is a challenge many farmers struggle with despite the fact that the vast majority of US farms still have more assets than debts. Though a farmer who is paying a mortgage may feel it's similar to paying rent, it is obviously very different. It makes more sense, in fact, to think of farmland debt as a savings or investment account a farmer must contribute to because with each payment, the farmer is not putting money directly in someone else's pocket (as renters are), but instead they are building equity that, in the future, they can turn back into cash. Over time, debt becomes wealth. Rent does not.

Additionally, Lyle's situation is unique because he was able to make peace with walking away from his farm. Many of his peers simply don't see that as an option and are more than willing to accept government payments to avoid doing so. Though American farmers are known for their fiercely independent and even libertarian mindsets, the industry has not shied away from (and has actively called for) high levels of taxpayer-funded financial entitlements, especially in recent years (AFBF 2020).

Perhaps most scandalously of all, it's not as if this redistribution of wealth to farmers is a victimless exercise. These payments redistribute wealth upwards, and wealthier farms are known to receive a larger share of federal payments than poorer farms (Edwards 2018). At the same time, federal subsidies in general have been proven not to have a significant effect on food prices either way (Smith et al 2017, 3), seemingly invalidating the argument that federal farm programs are an investment in food security. All of this means that despite taxpayers spending billions on farm programs annually, we're getting very little for it besides richer farmers.

The reality is the US has way more farmland in commodity grain production than it needs to meet the nutritional needs of Americans (Purdy 2018). Evidence that we're over-producing grain abounds, from the fact that we burn up billions of bushels of corn a year in fuel tanks to the creation of an entire meat production system that utilizes corn and soybeans for feed, despite the fact that ruminants, like cattle, experience significant adverse effects when they consume grain (Khafipour et al., 2016, 13). Essentially, in our mad rush to get rid of a tsunami of over-produced grains, we've shoved it into every available nook and cranny, whether it fit there or not.

A common remedy for this overproduction is global trade. Since we abhor the idea of regulating commerce on private land about as much as we hate letting farms go bankrupt, allowing farmers to farm what they want and selling their production overseas offers a politically beneficial out. The farm sector calls this "Feeding the World," an idea that was first encountered during World War II but didn't become common parlance until the late 1970s, when US overproduction started to get really out of control.

Exporting the US's excess grain worked for a while and managed to raise commodity prices, too, as demand from overseas sucked up extra grain. But that demand only motivated farmers to grow more and put more acres into production, which eventually drove the price down, incentivizing farmers to grow even more to make the same amount of revenue, inevitably prodding the system back to overproduction. This overproduction cycle, paired with global disruptions, led to devastating commodity price collapses in the late 1970s and early 1980s. Modern federal payment programs followed to bail out insolvent farms, the legacy of which we still contend with today (Widmar and Gloy 2015).

Though federal farm programs can slow this downward spiral, there's no evidence they do anything to unwind the system itself. The Farm Bill cannot undo the fact that agricultural land ownership has become increasingly concentrated in the hands of relatively few, and to keep it and monetize it efficiently, these farmers continue to grow larger and larger quantities of commodity grains, motivated by the same incentives that have existed for centuries. This is the system that's allowed farms like Clay's to thrive.

TOO BIG TO FOOD

Clay and Lyle have more in common than just their inclination toward commodities. In my conversations with them, they both expressed interest in doing something different, getting away from the roulette table of the commodity market, and maybe even growing some food for their local communities one day.

For Clay, however, that's not a simple proposition.

One of the most common questions the public asks about commodity grain production is "Why don't more farms produce more healthy food?" The answer offered is usually "Because subsidies make it more lucrative to grow commodity corn." Similarly, one of the most common explanations for why our diets have an over-abundance of cheap, commodity meat, highly processed foods, and high fructose corn syrup is that federal policies encourage and entrench commodity grain production. But these conversations are incomplete.

Clay is a good case study. He doesn't look at potentially producing fruit or vegetables on his land and dismiss it because it's more profitable to grow corn and soybeans due to program payments. Other factors are at play as well.

A key barrier for Clay to growing food crops is that he operates 3,500 acres of farmland. If Clay were to switch from growing corn and soybeans to fruits or vegetables, he would need 1/50th of the acres—if that. A few hundred acres of fresh produce is considered quite large for a produce farm, and would likely require hundreds of workers to plant, manage, harvest, pack and process the crop (Karst 2018; Rural Migration News 2020). Currently, Clay's farm is operated by four people, and his small town has the marketing infrastructure to take his grain and get him paid for it. Were he to decide to make the switch to a food crop, he'd have to gain the skills to grow it, make the capital investments of switching his equipment and facilities to accommodate it, find the labor to work it, and build the markets to deliver it to customers he currently doesn't have.

He might be able to get out of some of that by working with a produce distributor but doing so would eat into his potential revenue.

After making all those millions of dollars in investments, Clay will only be utilizing a few hundred of his 3,500 acres, unless of course he sold them to raise the capital to make the investments. It's important to remember that owning the land is the whole point for a lot of farmers. As Robert pointed out, farmland is a long-term investment, and holding as much of it as possible for as long as possible is the strategy. Plus, selling it would eliminate a reliable source of growing wealth, not to mention the emotional attachment between many farmers have to their land.

This exact trade-off, between desire to grow food but also to hold land, plays out as we might expect it to on many farms. Jennie Schmidt, for example, has focused on diversifying her crop mix in recent years. Driving to her place, about an hour and a half East of Washington, DC, her farm is a standout in a sea of corn and soybeans. Acres of tomatoes and green beans break up the trees, and I passed a vineyard that would not have been out of place in Napa.

The farm grows a wide variety of crops, including green beans, tomatoes, soybeans, corn, wine grapes, and even food-grade soybeans for tofu. The tofu contract was an exciting development for the farm because it allowed them to grow a crop using existing equipment but for a premium over commodity rates. To access the market, Jennie helped form a farmer cooperative that would grow what was needed for five or six Asian food processing companies in the region. But even with dedicated buyers, the coop only needs about two thousand acres of tofu beans annually, sourced from many farmers, so Jennie's farm only needs to grow a few dozen acres every year. That means she has to plant and sell other crops on thousands of other acres she co-owns and helps manage.

Even selling food-grade grains like soybeans, tomatoes for canning, green beans for freezing, and grapes to local and regional wineries, Jennie says more than a thousand acres of conventional corn and soybean production is what keeps the lights on at her place. Though the other revenue streams diversify the farm's income, they aren't particularly lucrative for an operation as geographically big as hers. Growing food, though important to her personally, is not the farm's money-maker.

So, a better answer to the question, "Why don't more farms grow food?" is, paradoxically, many farms own too much land to grow food. Often, if a commodity grain farmer wanted to instead pursue specialty crop production on their land (anything from nuts to berries to melons), doing so would require such a dramatic transformation of their business that, for many, it would feel (and cost) more like starting a whole new farm business from scratch.

Clay, even with his relatively progressive mindset and plans to move toward more food production and some more sustainable practices, also plans to keep nearly all of his farm's acres in commodity grain production for the foreseeable future.

THE KEY TO A SOLID GOLD JAIL CELL

Despite all that we know about farm income and wealth, it's still common to hear farmers claim they "have no choice" but to farm commodities, due to their size or a myriad of other reasons. But that idea implies they don't have the financial freedom to choose an alternative. We've seen, however, the vast majority of farmers do have the freedom and the agency to choose how and what they want to farm. Farmers are free to invest in growing their business in many different ways. They might change their crop mix, build a brand and sell directly to consumers, or add value by doing on-farm processing. A farmer who thinks they "have to" add acres and grow more commodity grain is not suffering from a lack of options, but from a lack of imagination.

The extraordinary irony of the "I have no choice but to grow grains" argument is that America's truly richest farmers do not grow commodity grains. This group includes, perhaps most famously, Stewart Resnick, the billionaire farmer who owns more than two hundred square miles of the state of California where he grows hundreds of thousands of acres of irrigated fruits and nuts that are sold under the Wonderful brand (Arax 2018). Though many billionaires who own farmland do so as an investment vehicle, Resnick is representative of the group that has grown and consolidated the high-value specialty crop space, selling branded fruits like Cuties that have become relatively ubiquitous in US supermarkets.

Compared to Clay's acres, Californian cropland is very different, with different productive potential and possible crops. But it's worth remembering that Iowa, the modern mecca of commodity grains, was one of the top US states for apple production in the early twentieth century (Priog and Tyndall 1999). So the Midwestern commodity grain grower's lament, that they have no choice but to grow corn, rings at least a little hollow.

The harvest of the US's commodity grain system has rarely been in doubt. Despite the industry's recurring obsession with the need to further expand to "feed the world," in reality we already produce more than enough calories to feed everyone on Earth (Holt-Giménez et al., 2012). Technology has allowed productivity to continue to outpace global demand for food, and Thomas Malthus's famous trap, where the limits of Earth's productive potential would create a cap on human population, has yet to manifest (Lueger 2019).

The recurring state of low commodity prices is also not unusual. This is by free market design. When commodity farmers complain about low prices, that isn't a temporary challenge that they need help to overcome; that's the status quo. So, if we are interested in supporting farmers through times of low commodity prices, we should do it with clear eyes, knowing it is not temporary assistance but something more like guaranteed income for a class of almost universally wealthy business owners.

At its core, growing commodity grain is a good way to keep a lot of land, earn money from it, and get the chance to do it mostly by yourself. It's a pretty sweet gig: working outside, no boss, lots of space to drive tractors, and guaranteed income so you don't have to worry much about whether anyone actually wants to buy what you grow.

These farms illustrate just how hard this model will be to unseat without intervention from far beyond the agricultural sphere. The scope of the problem is much bigger than previous discussions of the food system might have imagined. This conclusion can be overwhelming because it shows there is no easy solution to reducing or undoing agriculture's dependence on commodity crop production without bigger and more fundamental changes that go well beyond federal farm programs.

THE FARMER ABDICATES

Clay's progressive outlook has led him to skepticism about many of the "truths" of the commodity grain sector. One such "truth" is that there will always be strong domestic or international markets for corn and soybeans. Countries like Brazil and Argentina are becoming aggressive competitors, and after attending international trade missions to help build relationships with overseas grain buyers, Clay believes time is about up on the US's agricultural trade strategy.

"The EU, for example, they would buy as many non-GMO soybeans as we could grow," he says, "but we spend all of our efforts trying to convince them GMOs are safe instead. But shouldn't we just grow what the consumer wants, instead of growing what is easier for us and then trying to convince them it's safe?" Since demand for organics continues to out-pace production every year, Clay believes transitioning his operation toward 100 percent organic will allow him to take advantage of one of the biggest opportunities in grains. "I really think the only way to make decent money is diversi-fying your operation and finding higher value crops versus just traded commodities."

Clay's new farm business proposition is summed up in those two simple dictates, don't sell commodities, and grow what people want to buy. This logic has not only led him to adopt practices like cover cropping, conservation tillage, and rotating with livestock, it's also led him to venture into other crops, including yellow field peas, which are sold to make a plant-based protein powder, as well as organic field crops like corn that can go to feed organic livestock or for organic corn flour.

Clay's entrepreneurial outlook on his farming operation is laudable but not at all common. Among farmers I've spoken with, "growing the farm business" unanimously means one thing: more acres, more commodities, which only furthers the dreaded farm consolidation problem. Clay wants out of this acre accumulation spiral, so he plans to grow his farm not by expanding geographically, but by adding businesses. He plans to find new markets for unconventional crops, tell a great story about why his products are different so he can get away from charging commodity prices, and connect directly with consumers as much as he can.

What he's planning for his farm is certainly not easy work. Farmers, Clay included, like to be in the field more than anything else. But few people can say that they like every aspect of their job. Marketing, sales, logistics, business development, and strategy might not be as fun as driving equipment or raising livestock, but they're still vital elements of farm businesses and farmers must do them (or someone else must be paid to do it for them). In Clay's mind, growing a business was never supposed to be exclusively fun or easy work, and he's excited for the challenge.

Critically, Clay also has the resources to do it. His family farm has high income and wealth. Over the past twenty-five years or so, the farm has collected over $1.5 million in disaster aid, commodity, and conservation payments alone, even though corn prices were $7/bushel during that time (EWG Farm Subsidy Database 2020a). Clay didn't say exactly, but he told me he thinks this $1.5 million figure may actually be a significant undercount of what his farm has actually received.

In some ways, Clay's farm captures the look and feel of our Good Farm ideal, and in other ways it certainly doesn't. It's absolutely much larger and wealthier than we expected

Good Farms to be and doesn't grow the edible crops to feed the local community like we envision. Though Clay's planning to focus more on food production and environmental stewardship rather than on maximizing commodity grain production, his incentive to make that change quickly is limited. In other ways, Clay's farm achieves many things that, say, Robert's farm does not. It's economically stable and actually creates income that allows Clay to farm without impoverishing himself. It will almost without question be passed on to Clay and his brother's children if they want it, carrying the Govier farming legacy into the fourth generation.

As a result, I think it's safe to say the "rich" farm label also fails to help us identify the Good Farms we're looking for. Wealth definitely helps farmers support their families, maintain their farm across generations, and makes available more resources to invest in land and potentially conserve it. But a lot of money is made every year in American agriculture not by selling food, but by growing commodities, which leads to hard-to-justify externalities, and the taxpayer is often left holding the bag.

RICH FARMER, POOR FARMER

A couple of years ago, I came across a platitude that has helped guide my journey of understanding the farm wealth paradox: *Rich farmers grow food for poor people, and poor farmers grow food for rich people.*

In some ways, this phrase is accurate. Robert, Chris, and even Hannah's stories indicate that the expensive, "high-value" food we might buy at a specialty grocer or a farmers market is not necessarily providing the farmers who grow it with the comfortable income one might expect given the price. The point this idea misses is that income is only one tiny piece of the farm wealth equation. Earning a low income, as we've seen, does not necessarily make a farmer "poor."

At the same time, many stable and more successful farmers, those we'd consider "rich," are more likely to make their money growing commodity crops, which often end up in human diets in the form of highly processed foods. This commodity crop production, however, comes with a lot of unintended and costly consequences. Commodity corn is cheap, not because it's inexpensive to grow, but because it's heavily subsidized and many of the impacts of our extreme over-production are not paid by the farmers who grow it. Other commodities have their own unintended consequences, from commodity meat raised in confined animal feeding operations (CAFOs) to big commodity vegetable monocultures worked by exploited laborers. Perhaps the question is then whether it's possible to achieve the kind of scale that makes food affordable without the problems associated with commodity production.

Many believe the answer to that question is yes. They are optimistic that more sustainable and even regenerative practices, like those utilized by Chris Newman in Virginia, can be adopted at scale. The current problem with scaling operations with these tendencies is, as Chris pointed out, that farms don't come into the world fully grown. It takes time to scale up.

So, if there's somewhere to look now, where we might find our most thoughtful (and non-destructively) scaled farms, perhaps the factor to consider is not wealth or income, but age. Maybe it's the oldest farms that will be the best after all.

CHAPTER 4

SON OF A FARM

———

Sixteen generations ago, long before the United States became a nation, Nicholas Mills received a grant from the King of England to farm in the nascent colony of Virginia.

Today, the Mills family continues to farm that land.

I met J.N. Mills, Nicholas's many times great grandson, on a sultry summer day, standing among Trump/Pence-stickered pickups in the farm's driveway. He was wearing big, thick glasses and a plaid button up that fit snugly over his barrel of a chest. He was bulky in a way that only old farmers achieve, like layers of hotdogs and apple pie had been draped over the form of a bodybuilder.

When he first mentioned being a sixteenth-generation farmer, I started doing the math in my head. Over that time, the farm outlasted two wars fought right here in Virginia. It saw slavery and a civil war come and go (and likely participated in both, though I didn't ask), withstood world wars and the New Deal, adopted and adapted steel and horses right through to million-dollar combines. For all those years, the Mills family was here planting seeds, tending crops, and bringing in the harvest.

The name of the original Mills' farm was Pleasant Level, which according to the sign was established in 1695. J.N.'s wife Darlene showed me an original transcript of the grant that gave a four-hundred-acre parcel to Nicholas Mills in 1725 for the cost of forty shillings, which in the year 1730 was worth an equivalent of about twenty days wages or about $320 modern USD (UK National Archives 2021). The same parcel of agricultural land is likely worth about $1.9 million today (USDA NASS 2020b).

The grant outlined the tax that Nicholas would owe to the Colony and Dominion of Virginia, and in turn promised his heirs and successors would be entitled to this land forever. King George would surely have been happy to see his promises had been kept faithfully down to the sixteenth generation of Mills farmers, though I bet he'd be disappointed to learn that by the third and fourth generations, the family were no longer English subjects.

What would it feel like, I wondered, *to have the weight of sixteen generations of legacy behind you?*

"I was born on the farm," J.N. told me that first day. "It's a way of life as much as a profession, and it's something I've enjoyed doing all my life. My son, my family—same thing. They've always wanted to be on the farm. It's in our blood."

I spent that first day with J.N. touring the farm, and as we passed, he pointed out the home he shares with his wife, and those of his son and his family, his mother, his niece and her family, and his brother, brother-in-law, and nephew. Four generations of Mills, representing the fifteenth, sixteenth, seventeenth, and eighteenth incarnations, were simultaneously working and calling the farm home.

THE PRICE OF IMMORTALITY

The multigenerational farmer has a special power over our psyches. The idea that farmers have the work "in their blood" plays on our craving for a destiny, a higher purpose. In that way, multi-generational farmers live in our imaginations as living time capsules, preserving the knowledge and traditions of the past for our collective benefit, securing our practical, land-based heritage on our behalf. A fifth, tenth, or sixteenth generation farmer is assumed to have a deep intimacy with the ethic of our agrarian past. Maybe that's what makes our oldest farms the Good Farms after all?

If the Mills farm is any indication, however, America's longest operating farms are not the simplistic and bucolic ones of our dreams.

Over the centuries, the Mills farm has grown and changed considerably. What was in 1725 just four hundred acres in Hanover county is now about 5,500. Besides the 3,600 acres of cropland dedicated to commodity soybeans, corn, sorghum, and wheat, it also includes a few hundred acres each of working forest, pasture and hay fields, and wetlands. In our drive around the farm, we passed field after field of Mills' crops, mostly tall green wheat, that had been planted the previous winter and would soon be ready for harvest, but also some young corn and just the first sprigs of sorghum.

"We can grow most any crop," J.N. explained, "but we have to have a market for it. No need growing something if you can't sell it." Like Clay, the Mills are always looking for ways to avoid participating in unpredictable commodity markets. They grow hard red wheat and barley, though it's not destined for the local flour mill but for a seed company who will sell it to other farmers—earning the farm above-commodity prices. Despite these efforts, corn remains the king crop on the Mills farm. They grow standard dent corn and ship it off to a nearby ethanol plant to be turned into fuel. For these efforts, the Mills farm has collected at least $3 million in farm program payments over the past twenty-five years (EWG Farm Subsidy Database 2021b).

It wasn't long ago that the Mills farm grew food crops like watermelons, but those days are now just a memory. J.N. tells me the farm use to do some "truck farming," or small-scale specialty crop production (industry jargon for fruits, vegetables, nuts, and flowers), where the produce is then sold relatively directly into retail markets.

"There's a lot of truck farms around here, but you can't make any money doing it," J.N. says, "they might sell to some local stores or restaurants, or at farmers markets or something, but there's no money in it, and it's hard work. Hard on the body." In other words, when the Mills came up against the same financial puzzle Georgie did, they too walked away. The farm does still raise about 150 cow-calf pairs who roamed the pastures we passed, grazing on the thick carpet of grass. The calves will be sold at auction when the price is right or the farm needs the cash, adding new meaning to the phrase "stock options." But the bovines aren't the only thing in those fields that could be monetized.

"We cut some small square hay bales because people have a lot of horses around here." The corners of J.N.'s mouth turn up as he tells me this, glancing at me out of the corner of his eye. "We call those horses 'lawn ornaments,' 'cause that's all they are. Folks buy 'em thinking 'I'm gonna learn to ride.' Well, that lasts about a year. But after that, they still need feeding, so we cut them small square bales anyway." In that way, even feeding the neighborhood equine pets fits into the farm's financial plan. All of this helps with diversification, J.N. explains, because it makes sure there's always something around for the farm to sell.

In the last century, most farmers moved away from this relatively diversified kind of operation to focus on large-scale commodity grain production. The Mills farm is no exception. Like Jennie's farm in Maryland, the cattle, hay, and other secondary income streams are helpful in a pinch, but commodity grain is the farm's money-maker. Without the vast majority of acres, time, and attention dedicated to modern crops like GMO corn and soybeans, there would be no Mills farm today.

This gets to the heart of why our farmer-as-time capsule assumption is flawed. The Mills farm hasn't survived for hundreds of years because it has clung rigidly to tradition. It has survived by adapting, and by ensuring every one of the farm's acres pays.

Loving the work is surely important to J.N. and his family, but the farm's long history it a testament to their understanding that love is not enough. Financial stability is the key to farm longevity, and the Mills don't take that for granted.

MINE THE FARM

Farm longevity is clearly dependent on financial stability, but it's also dependent on environmental stability. If the soil blows away, the water runs out, or pests dominate, farming becomes impossible, right? It's hard to understand, then, why an operation like the Mills farm, with ample resources and a goal to continue for many more generations, would not be moving quickly away from the extractive practices of commodity grain farming that threaten its long-term ecological integrity (Food Print, n.d.).

A common idea in the agricultural world is that "farmers are the original environmentalists" (Western Growers 2020). Behind this trope is an assumption that because land is privately held, landowners have the best incentives to improve soil health, protect water from harmful chemicals, and maintain the elements of the property (like the forests and wildlife habitats) their family has treasured for generations. Not just because they want to, this argument goes, but because their livelihood—their ability to continue farming—depends on it.

The Mills are certainly utilizing some methods that fall under the heading of sustainability practices. They use conservation tillage equipment to minimize soil disturbance and rotate crops between seasons. They also plant cover crops to help prevent nutrient leakage away from the field, and more importantly, to save money by keeping costly fertilizer where it belongs.

In adopting even these few practices, the Mills are leaders in the farm community. Consider the practice of planting cover crops, which has many known benefits for a farm's bottom line, not to mention that existing programs will pay farmers to do it (Clark 2012, 9; SARE, n.d.). The Mills use cover crops because they know the practice offers meaningful return on investment. Yet only 3.9 percent of total cropland acres in the US were planted in cover crops as of 2017 (Zulauf and Brown 2019).

If cover crops provide any indication of whether farmers writ large are uniquely motivated, by virtue of owing land, to adopt practices that improve the land's long-term quality, this trend does not bode well. Though rates of conservation tillage practices are increasing more rapidly, other sustainable ag practices like rotational grazing and use of alternatives to commercial fertilizers have actually decreased overall in recent years (NSAC 2019).

Beyond these marginal sustainability practices, however, the Mills run a standard commodity farm. They utilize chemical fertilizers and pesticides, irrigate, use heavy equipment for planting, spraying, and harvesting, and grow large, single-crop acreages of genetically modified grains. Each of these practices is known to have negative long-term impacts on soil quality, and therefore land value (Food Print, n.d.).

So why are these farmers making the seemingly nonsensical decision to degrade farmland for short-term gain when proven alternatives are available? Christine Su, the agtech expert, says this is another version of the "farmers are in the real estate business" reality. Remember farmers operate two businesses, a farmland-holding real estate business and a farm production business, and it's in balancing the trade-offs between these two businesses where a farmer might make non-optimal decisions. Christine says many farmers don't acknowledge that they own land that can either be improved or degraded over the long term, which causes them to act against their own interest.

In effect, the vast majority of commercial farmers act as agricultural production companies. They prioritize getting the most crop out of the ground, and in doing so they often use extractive tools and practices. That might look like a good short-term decision because it creates more income with relatively minimal cost to the land each year. However, it doesn't make sense *for the farm real estate business* to, for example, degrade soil quality or increase flood potential because doing so affects the value of farmland (Johnson 2020). In other words, degrading land to extract maximum yields is a bad decision for a farm real estate company, but not necessarily for a farm production company.

When farmers prioritize short-term gains in the production business, they are mining the long-term value of the land. Perhaps farmers do this because they don't realize that this is the effect extractive practices have, or perhaps they're making a conscious choice of cash now over high-quality, high-value land in the future. One thing is clear: a farmer's financial health certainly doesn't "depend on" their land maintaining peak environmental health. In fact, it's possible to make a lot of money degrading and eventually exhausting land.

The short-term gains and relatively low short-term cost of extractive practices explains why many farmers are not interested in changing their farming practices, even when it's in their long-term financial interest. It's not that these farmers can't afford to farm differently, more often it's simply that extraction is more lucrative. Not to mention that new practices often require more management effort and might include more short-term risks than the alternative.

HAVE YOUR FARM AND EAT IT, TOO

Evidence that something more complex than "farmers are environmentalists" abounded on another visit to the Mills farm. As J.N. and I drove through a hilly soybean field in his pickup, he explained that the field on either side of the road used to be a forest and over the past decade the farm had "reclaimed" it, and over four hundred other acres, from the woods. By way of explanation, he simply said, "God isn't making new land anymore, so if you want to farm more, it's got to come from somewhere."

Commodity grain farmers in the US are almost always looking to farm more land. It's not unreasonable; we live in a growth-centric economy, which means it's not enough to continue growing the same crops on the same land for hundreds of years. To grow their incomes to match things like rising costs of living, farmers have to grow their businesses. In US farming, this growth is almost always measured in more total production. In some cases, this increased production can be achieved by growing crops on existing land more efficiently, for example, by getting more bushels per acre using improved fertilizers or better genetics. Eventually though, the productive maximum of a parcel of land is reached. At this point, farmers feel they have to look to new acres by either buying or renting them from neighbors or, in the case of the Mills farm, converting land from alternative uses to cropland.

It's not just the desire for more crop acres that motivates deforestation on farms though. There are also more direct financial benefits to chopping down trees. I witnessed this revenue opportunity up close during my first visit to a logging site on the Mills farm.

The high-pitched whine and earth-trembling thuds were heard and felt before we could see them. As the scene came into view through the pickup's windshield, I spied a burly man in a machine deftly maneuvering a giant claw as it gripped a thirty-foot-long felled tree, swinging it around to the stripper, dragging it over blades that trimmed off all the branches and leaves in seconds, and then flung the clean log around to rest in the bed of a waiting semi-truck. It would have felt cartoonish watching these majestic trees get stripped down to their underwear, if not for the intensity of the sounds that signaled life and limb were in danger as tons of wood moved through the air.

While we watched, the semi's engine rumbled to life. With a bed full of freshly harvested logs, it headed for the sawmill a few miles up the county. Timber, I realized, was as much a crop as anything else on the farm. Every acre of land the Mills own makes money, without exception.

In other ways, too, the Mills are going out of their way to earn money on their land. A few miles down the road from the logging site, J.N. called my attention to a low-lying wooded area dotted with young trees and shrubs. It's a wetland, he explained, one of many on the farm.

"We created these wetland banks; they're constructed." This is a new revenue stream for the farm. The wetlands are built on relatively poor former cropland, and for every acre of approved wetlands they build, they can sell offset credits to construction companies and others who negatively impact other wetlands in Virginia. Purchasing these offset credits is required by law, ostensibly because if a company is damaging wetlands in one area, purchasing the offsets allows them to pay for the creation or maintenance of wetlands elsewhere (Stephenson et al., 2016).

Beyond the wetlands, the farm has even leased a few hundred acres to a local solar power project. In these ways, the farm is financially diversified while also creating some ecological benefits.

In light of these efforts, it would be misleading to say that maintaining the land's natural integrity is a top motivator on the Mills farm, and I don't think J.N. thinks of himself as much of an environmentalist. Instead, the idea that there's "no point in growing something we don't have a market for" wins out. If there's a market for wetlands, the Mills will grow them. If there's a market for logs and for more cropland (and there always is), then the farm's rich carbon sinks will be cut down, sold, and planted in commodity grains. If neighboring communities demand solar energy, the Mills will happily lease out a hundred acres of marginal pasture-land at good market rates to help make it happen. If conservation tillage and cover crops reliably raise yields without becoming too much of an inconvenience, they'll stay in the playbook, alongside use of chemical fertilizer and pesticides and mono-culture grain crops spanning thousands of acres.

The one thing that's undeniable about the Mills farm is that it certainly is not a time capsule. For being a grandfatherly gentleman, J.N.'s proficiency at navigating farms weather apps, his knowledge of the latest trends and technologies in agriculture, and his ability to recognize the potential in something like a solar power project without getting hung up on the politics sets him apart as distinctly adaptive and forward-thinking among his peers. This, I think, is the key to the Mills farm's longevity. Over the course of sixteen generations, it survived because its owners did not cling to the past for its own sake or insist on tradition when tradition no longer served them. The Mills are pragmatic farm business owners following markets where they lead, making conservative decisions with an eye to growing wealth, and exploring new trends when the money is right. In that way, J.N. is on the cutting edge of American farms.

What's more, J.N.'s farm is the only place he'd want to be. For him, it's the ideal job. He's surrounded by family, busy at times, but not so busy he can't take a day off here and there to drive around the farm with a reporter. And the money is good, enough to support him, his wife, his brother and his wife, their two sons and their families, to pay for trips to farm conferences and annual vacations to beaches in North Carolina, and even to feed a "lawn ornament" of their own.

For J.N., his farm is his past, present, and future; and he and his forebears put every acre of it to work to ensure it stays that way.

THE WEIGHT OF A FARM

Agriculture and the idea of destiny have long been tied up in each other, and it makes sense. If destiny is life following a set plan to fulfill a larger purpose, that's exactly what a farm is—a set of plans and intentions that shapes a natural system to a human end.

Of course, destiny has a dark side. If a farmer has it "in their blood" to tame the wilderness, to plant seeds in neat rows, or to mate animals for selective progeny, then doing this work is not just a job or a business, it's a birthright. The land a farmer owns, in this case, is not so much an asset used to operate their business, or even a treasured possession like a family heirloom. It's a need, the tool by which to access their identity as a higher order being, one with the power to make and create plant and animal life, ostensibly for the continuation of human life. This craving is validated and rewarded by our common admiration of multi-generational farms.

Many farmers do see their role as agriculturalist as a central part of their identity, which is a key reason why talking about farm economics, policy, or business objectively can be so uncomfortable in farming spheres. There's a clear problem, though, with "farmer" as an identity. What if you were born into a farming family, but don't want to farm? What if you do want to farm, but you're not good at it? When a job becomes a destiny, many farmers feel they can't just walk away, and they feel incredible emotional and psychological pressure to preserve their farms at nearly any cost.

One farmer I spoke to about this pressure is Mike, who shared his story with me but requested I not use his name due to the emotional sensitivity he still feels. He grew up on a family farm in Colorado and spent most of his life working it.

"One of my biggest fears was I would be the asshole who lost it," he told me first by phone, "and I think I feared that throughout my lifetime of farming." This fear began, he said, at the very beginning. He started farming right after high school with his dad, but due to interpersonal conflicts, he left after a few years to start his own farm. He purchased 2,400 acres a few counties over. He and his wife raised two kids there and made it a home. They went on to survive many low-income years in the 1980s, though not without the battle scars of debt.

Eventually his father asked him to come back and buy the family farm from him, and feeling the duty to legacy, he decided to walk away from the farm he'd built and return to the family operation. He farmed there for years, making the financials work as best he could, fighting daily with that fear that he would be the one to lose the farm.

"In 2000, we had an offer on the farm we really couldn't refuse," he said. "If I had turned it down, I'd have been the fool." He took the offer and sold the farm.

Most farms, like most small businesses, close eventually. Many farmers don't want to die working; they want to retire and reap the rewards of their labor, like anyone else. Not all farmers have children or grandchildren who feel that same call to legacy that Mike felt, so some end up selling the businesses to strangers. Some farms exit through bankruptcy too, unable to make the financials work. The path to coming to terms with exiting a family farm and separating it from oneself can be a long and lonely road.

It's worth considering though that elsewhere in the world of startups and small businesses we tend to honor exiting, especially through the sale of a business. Exiting is often the only way for an entrepreneur to recoup their full financial and labor investment, and in most business sectors in the US, we tend to have appreciation and tolerance for failure, too (Burchell and Hughes 2006). The fact that we abhor exiting in farming, especially through failure, is odd. Farming is a high-risk business, and everything we know about business tells us that when risk is high, potential reward is also high (which is also true in farming). We believe entrepreneurs should be rewarded for taking risks that pay off, and they shouldn't be unduly punished when they don't. Yet our aversion to farm failures remains, despite the fact that any other small business in the US is more than twenty times more likely to fail than a farm (US SBA Office of Advocacy, n.d., 2; Neeley 2019).

I asked Mike what it meant to him to sell his family farm. His answer surprised me.

"I really felt that load come off my shoulders...and I just had a smile on my face because there was no debt." Now Mike lives in New Mexico. He's retired. Despite all the fear he felt throughout his life of losing the farm, the weight of the debt, or in other words the weight of keeping the farm, was even more painful.

"I think it takes some maturity," he said, "to finally figure out that maybe your happiness is more important than your family heritage." Mike also points out that though the farm was actually his mother's family farm historically, when he told her he planned to sell it she was relieved. "She goes,

'Oh, we can finally break it, we can finally break that mold.'"
I asked Mike whether there was anything that could have gotten him to stay in farming in the end.

"I would have liked to win the lottery so I could have kept farming until all that was gone, too," he told me with a smile in his voice, noting that I'd probably heard that before, and I have.

Of course, for many farms, that break is not so painless. Robert expressed plenty of existential dread when I pressed him on the possibility of leaving his farm behind.

"What else am I gonna do?" he asked me, a shrug in his voice, "I have the entire weight of my family's history on me. I'm very susceptible to that. I come from a family of people that enshrine their forebears, for better or worse. I have to avoid the nostalgia trap as much as possible, which is a real, toxic thing for anyone." Robert says he tries not to let nostalgia affect him, but sometimes it's unavoidable. "It's not necessarily the romance, it's that I have allowed it to become a part of my identity that's very valuable to me and trying my hardest to make it work is something I have to do." Robert is certainly not alone in believing farming or ranching is their destiny.

All these conversations got me thinking about the interplay between jobs and destiny. *Do I think I was destined to be a journalist?* I wondered. The answer is a resounding no. Despite whatever aptitude I might have for the work, it can be a struggle, and though I love it, I can absolutely foresee a future where it makes sense to leave it behind. One of the many differences between my professional experience and J.N.'s or Robert's is not only that they believe their job is their destiny, but many of the rest of us believe (hypocritically) that their job is their destiny, too.

A SECOND-HAND JOB

At the end of our conversation, Mike offered some insight on what it means to be the son of a farmer, describing his own sense of relief that his son would not have to take over the farm.

"My daughter was never interested in the farm," Mike said, "and my son, at that time, said 'I'm never coming back to the farm.' Then once we sold it, he was very upset for probably a year. I think, it kind of struck this nerve because it was his crutch. Like if he didn't succeed at what he was doing, he could always go back to the farm."

The idea of returning to the family farm as a crutch for farm kids resonated with my experience. Though I've certainly met many farm kids who always wanted to farm, who love the work, and are joyful in carrying on their family legacy, I've also met many farmers who farm for reasons similar to what Mike described. Some farm because they didn't really like college. Maybe they worked at the local equipment dealership or another business in town for a few years, but finding they disliked their boss or being an employee, their coworkers, the work itself, or the way they were evaluated on it, they opted to work for their dad instead.

None of these, however, are good reason to farm or to start or take over any kind of business. Having competencies, grit, social skills, and emotional intelligence, being able to respond to deadlines and follow rules, whether set by your boss or a teacher, are all important skills. When a farm kid knows they can always return to their family's farm, however, it can become an excuse for young people to avoid the often-painful process of gaining those abilities.

Selling the farm, Mike says, took that crutch away from his son and forced him to stand on his own with no safety net. Today his son has a good job, and most importantly he's happy. "And no one gutted him into farming," Mike says.

For these reasons, it's important for the rest of us to remember that there is no evidence that farming is genetic. Consider how comfortable you would be seeing a doctor if, rather than having attended medical school and passing a board certification, he was simply the son and grandson of a doctor. How excited would you be to hire a lawyer or a plumber who, having had no requirement to receive formal training in their field and no mechanism by which to identify and remove bad actors, simply claims they deserve your trust because of the many generations their family has been actively practicing? Why should farming, work that impacts not just our food but also the health of the environment, require any less rigorous evaluation of its practitioners?

None of this is meant to diminish the advanced and important skills needed to farm well, or to say a farmer necessarily needs formal education or training to be a talented farm business owner and operator. But I think it's at least safe to wonder whether simply growing up in and around a business is enough training to understand everything needed to run the business and to build all the skills necessary to run it well.

Even if we agree that it is, arguably there should be a mechanism to remove ineffective or harmful farmers (like a lawyer can be disbarred or a doctor can have their license revoked). Given that we know inadequate and even actively bad farmers exist and continue operating relatively unimpeded, this seems like a necessity to protect public resources that farmers might affect, like air and water, or public funds like farm program payments. In another sector, market forces might work to put poor-performing farmers out of business, but in the agriculture industry, it's possible to access benefits without being a successful farmer. A family farm could stay in business for decades on tax benefits alone, even while running the day-to-day operations of food and fiber production ineptly, and possibly degrading land and public resources while they're at it.

GOOD OL' FARMS

Though the average age of the American farmer is well-known, both statistically and in our imaginations (it's about fifty-eight years old) the average age of the American multi-generation farm remains a mystery (Zulauf 2020, 1). In fact, because the Census of Agriculture focuses on the farmers and not the farm, it's not possible for researchers to track the lifespan of farm businesses when it crosses generations (Key and Roberts 2007). So, we can't do much generalizing about whether farms with longer lifespans are healthier financially or environmentally than younger operations.

Given this, and the stories we've examined, I think it's hard to argue that multi-generational farms hold any kind of special claims to being the farms of our agrarian ideal, either in terms of the way they operate or the markets they serve. Our Good Farm vision of a historical farm that has changed little over the years is outdated.

In many ways, the Mills farm is not so different from Clay's other than being a bit bigger and more well established. The Mills farm is a leader among its peers, utilizing many laudable practices, but compared to the Good Farm of our dreams, which is focused on feeding families and protecting the integrity of the land, it falls short. Multigenerational farms, then, are not defined by how many people they feed or how much land they preserve. They are defined by pragmatism, which allows them to adapt to changing times and hang on to land wealth and continue to grow. That adaptation is not about maintaining agrarian virtue, it's about pursuing personal and familial financial goals.

That laser focus on profitability and wealth accumulation, in many cases, has helped old farms achieve stability. This stability looks like the perpetuation of inherited wealth. Legacy farms are celebrated in the US as great achievements, and in many ways they are. But rarely do we reckon with what they represent, namely the passing of massive amounts of private wealth from generation to generation in a way not dissimilar from a trust fund.

To some perhaps that might not register as a problem. We love to hear how many years a farm has been in a family. We are less happy to acknowledge this is a celebration of entrenched wealth, passed from farmer to farmer not based on farming talent but based on the accident of birth. In that way, our farm system is a monarchy and not a democracy, with all the attendant issues. Compound this genetic farm lottery with the ways our national history—which is lousy with racial- and gender-discriminatory farmland giveaways— has impacted the accumulation of wealth, and the system of inter-generational farming starts to look terribly rigged in favor of a few.

This reality has made it so that if a new farmer doesn't have generations of inherited wealth at their back, building a successful farm that is a good place to live and work is almost impossible. Expressing frustration about the difficulty of "making it" as a beginning farmer and sadness about the challenge of farmland access, and in the next breath, congratulating those who fell into the profession and their land, is self-defeating. If we want to see a diverse, growing field of farmers, then we have to stop rewarding and obsessing over farmer pedigrees.

Maybe, then, the Good Farms we're looking for won't be found among the ranks of America's oldest farms but are instead relative newcomers. Maybe it's not the last generation of farms, but the first, that embodies the spirit of our proudest pastoral traditions.

CHAPTER 5

100% THAT FARM

"I call myself an accidental farmer," Debbie Morrison explained, a hint of exasperation in her voice. "If you had asked me five years ago if I'd be making hard cider, I'd have told you, 'You're nuts.' If you would have asked me twenty years ago if I'd be an organic farmer, I'd have again told you, 'You're nuts,' but you know, it just sort of happened."

Debbie, with her husband Jim, are the farmers at Sapsucker Farms in Mora, Minnesota, about an hour North of Minneapolis. They grow apples to make cider, as well as maple trees for syrup, chickens, and fruits, vegetables, and mushrooms in an organic-certified market garden.

Debbie and Jim did not come from farm backgrounds. They bought their 172 acres in the late '90s while both were still working in the Minneapolis-St. Paul area. The farm had been dormant for half a century, and there was no house on the property. That was fine by them because in the beginning they had no intention of farming. They were just outdoorsy people looking for a weekend getaway.

"In 2000, we decided we wanted to live up here," Debbie told me by phone, "so we built the house and moved, but I continued to commute down to Minneapolis for work." Their first big project after building the house was to convert forty acres of pasture into native prairie, complete with seven-foot-tall bluestem grasses. They were even able to get the USDA's Natural Resources Conservation Service to help cover most of the cost. A few years later, inspired by their success, they decided to add an apple orchard to their new prairie.

Not long after establishing the apple trees, Debbie decided to quit the corporate world to run the farm full-time. She started with a simple, apple and garden vegetable-based Community Supported Agriculture membership (CSA), which was a demanding project. When they began experimenting with cider-making and the Yellow Belly brand took off, they decided to quit the CSA for a while to focus on the new endeavor.

Today, the farm's Yellow Belly Cider is an award-winning beverage made right on the farm from their organic apples. It's available as far afield as Utah, but it's mostly consumed at the farm's tasting room. The winery (technically, fermented fruit juices are considered wines) is now a place where people can hike, bring the whole family for a picnic, and spend a peaceful afternoon. Having added non-alcoholic farm-made beverages to their menu, from ginger ale to kombucha, the farm is now fully a production business *and* an outdoor experience destination.

The changes have been good for both the business and the community. The farm no longer grows enough apples to fill their need for cider-making, so they source apples from their neighbors.

"We have maybe four or five farmers now that are planting apple trees, and not only does that give other people a market, it also helps mitigate our risk. Because if we get hit by a major hailstorm and lose all of our apples, it's okay if there's another farmer down the road here that can supply them, which means they also get to share in the reward." Debbie has also introduced a re-imagined CSA, which is now monthly instead of weekly, includes cider and other value-added products, and requires shareholders to come to the farm for pick-up.

Debbie says with all the products the farm sells, it's doing quite well.

"From a tax standpoint," she told me discretely, "farms are complicated because everything here could be considered an expense. But let's just say it's a cash flow-positive situation. It's paying its bills, we're keeping everybody happy, and we're not strained financially."

HAVE YOU SEEN THIS FARMER?

If you're anything like me, hearing Debbie's story is a relief. *This*, I thought, *is the farm I've been looking for.* Not only is it financially stable, but it also has its roots buried deep in ideas like native ecosystem preservation, community development, and making high quality products people want. Perhaps it truly is the new farmers who will save us.

But how common is Sapsucker's experience generally among beginning farmers? The short answer is we don't really know.

The broad strokes we can take away from the Census of Ag are that beginning producers make up about 25 percent of farm operators in the US. About 75 percent of those report their primary occupation to be something other than farming (in other words, they have a day job), and just 6 percent report specializing in fruits like apples, tree nuts, or berries. The majority of these beginning farmers have access to fifty or fewer acres and farm in coastal states (USDA NASS 2020a). According to these statistics, then, Debbie and Jim's experience is not common at all.

But as we previously discussed, the Census of Ag has its limitations. First of all, according to USDA Debbie and Jim are no longer beginning farmers. Despite their first generation-farm status and their late-career start, the "beginning farmer" label is reserved for those with less than ten years of experience operating a farm business (Key and Lyons 2019).

The Census's blind spots extend further. Researchers have found it often takes years for USDA to identify and count beginning farmers. They predict as many as forty to fifty thousand beginning farmers may have gone unreported in the 2012 Census due to this phenomenon, which would have doubled the number of beginning farmers counted (Katchova and Ahearn 2017). To wit, an informal survey of the beginning farmers in this book reveals few of them have ever participated in the Census of Agriculture.

We are knowingly wading into that information gap where little is reliably understood about the state of young and beginning farm businesses--how they start, who they are, and why they fail--beyond the broadest trends.

Even the broadest of these trends can be misleading. We know the Census of Ag is ineffective in parsing the different reasons why people start farms. The data does not differentiate between people who are simply interested in rural property ownership, those who farm as a hobby, and those who are trying to make a living growing crops (Rosenberg 2017). So, among the hundreds of thousands of operators in the 2017 Census who identify as having farmed for fewer than ten years, we can't tell how many are like Debbie and how many are simply new rural landowners.

Exacerbating this problem is the fact the USDA changed its survey methodology between the 2012 and 2017 censuses in an effort to capture a more complete picture of the people working in the farm sector. Unfortunately, that change makes analyzing the figures across these years difficult because it's hard to tell with certainty how much of the changes among the young farmer population in those five years was simply a result of a different survey method (Rosenberg 2017).

IF YOU BUILD IT

So, we're left wondering, what made Sapsucker work when so many other new farms we've visited didn't?

My first guess was that it's because they've figured out how to market farm products like raw fruits and vegetables, value-added products like cider, and events and atmosphere at all at once. I hypothesized this diversification of products and lines of business must have made it easier to survive the early stages of farming and get to the financial stability they currently enjoy.

The experience of a mother-daughter team of lavender farmers made me think the benefits of this work might not be as direct and obvious for others as they've been for Jim and Debbie at Sapsucker Farms.

I first met Mary and Allison Horseman of the Woodstock Lavender Company in the Library of Congress where they were showcasing their lavender sachets, lotions, and lip balms to members of Congress and their staffs. They were invited there to represent the state of Kentucky as a small business pushing the state's agriculture forward. Mary and Allison grow several hundred perennial lavender plants and harvest the herb for use in culinary and bath and body products.

"We're selling a product that is unique," Allison told me later by phone. "We're handcrafting it, and we're doing it in small batches ourselves. But you can also go to Target or Big Lots and buy lavender-scented bath salts. So, we have to really convey what makes our product different and better." Processing their lavender into higher value products, in other words, might help in collecting more revenue than selling raw lavender, but the extra revenue potential also attracts fiercer competitors.

Allison and Mary have also ventured into the world of agrotourism, hosting lavender-themed teas on their farm and welcoming guests to dine among the plants on menus filled with lavender-inclusive dishes. They've been a big hit, Allison says, but it's a lot of work. It's a whole separate business on top of the existing one, and they've been particularly hard on Allison and her family. With small children around and a partner that works off the farm, giving up nights and weekends to welcome strangers onto the property is tough.

"People don't realize 'visiting a farm' entails so much prep work," she wrote later in an email, "like continual maintenance, rental fees (for things like portable restrooms), insurance, and so, so, so much time. It honestly takes a lot of people (or a higher cost) to make it worthwhile to have people on the farm." For all these reasons, Allison expects these events will stay limited for the foreseeable future.

Currently, Allison and Mary do most of the farm's work themselves, from executing on-farm events to planting, tending, and harvesting, to creating and testing products. Managing the level and diversity of work can be grueling, Allison says, because to get from a lavender bush to a product in the customers hands takes dozens of steps and a huge range of skills. Currently, these two women take on this intense work without being able to pay themselves a living wage in exchange.

In Allison's mind, getting the farm to be a more profitable place where a living wage might be possible would require more lavender plants, more products, more events, and competing in even larger markets. But each of those steps requires even more labor, which they currently can't afford. Plus, despite several years of effort, these first-time lavender growers are still just trying to perfect the actual growing of lavender, which creates its own limitations to growth.

Allison is still optimistic, but she recognizes the farm has a long way to go to reach a sustainable level of profitability. Selling consumer goods comes with a lot of fixed costs, from packaging and raw materials to labor and overhead, meaning margins for error are minuscule, and even in the best of times, profit potential is small. Unlike Jim and Debbie, Allison and Mary didn't have the resources or capacity to retool their whole farm to focus on outdoor experiences when the pandemic hit. Whereas rapidly changing consumer habits were an opportunity to attract a new audience to Sapsucker, the Woodstock Lavender Company was stalled by pandemic changes. Though they've been resilient in making many changes since, and have even increased their online sales, the future of their business is still in limbo.

All in all, Allison and Mary's experiences indicate that selling higher value products and coordinating on-farm events aren't, in themselves, keys to unlocking financial success.

IT'S THE ECOLOGY, STUPID

My next guess as to the secret of Sapsucker's success is that perhaps it stems directly from their environmental care. "Regenerative" practices, some have argued, allow farmers to earn premium prices and profits, and they also reduce farm input costs and improve the quality of land (LaCanne and Lundgren 2018), perhaps leading to the kind of financial sustainability Sapsucker has achieved.

Excited journalists and farmers have been expounding the Earth-saving benefits of regenerative farming for years now. From environmental groups and green-leaning politicians to Silicon Valley technologists, the list of people who believe regenerative farming will not only transform agriculture, but also the world, continues to grow (Payne 2019).

In many ways, Sapsucker Farms is the embodiment of the ideal regenerative farm. Debbie and Jim invested first in reinvigorating native prairies and then added another perennial crop (apple trees) that can be monetized not by pushing for maximum yields and extracting from the land, but by converting their harvest into something that can help the business earn more money. The prairie attracts pollinators and helps keep the farm's insect ecosystem in balance so harsh pesticide use can be avoided, and both the prairie grasses and the apple trees store significant amounts of carbon over time (Meyer and Weisenhorn 2019). Plus, all the farming at Sapsucker is certified organic, which adds value both to the food it produces and to the farm-visitor experience.

I talked to Dr. Ricardo Salvador, an expert in agronomy and Director of Food and Environment programs at the Union of Concerned Scientists, about whether these regenerative practices might be the key to Sapsucker overcoming the economics of farming. He came to the realization that the agricultural industry's standard extractive practices fail to account for the costs they incur to Earth's natural systems, and he has been advocating for sustainable and regenerative practices ever since.

"Soil formation, for instance, the water cycle, nutrient cycles, biodiversity, the interaction between beneficial and predatory pests, and so on—those things aren't priced in[to] the farm economy," Ricardo told me as we chatted in his office in 2019. He says this means the price we pay for food (and the market price of commodities) simply doesn't include the true environmental cost of growing crops.

"Conventional [farming] systems degrade or reduce biodiversity. They erode or contaminate soil. They reduce surface water quality. They generate greenhouse gas emissions. But you can be a successful farmer while you're doing all that because none of that costs you directly, and you're not docked [for it] when you sell your cotton or your wheat." It was the backlash to this distorted economy, he says, that led to the notions of sustainable and then regenerative agriculture. In Ricardo's mind, conventional farming has a limited future, dependent on how quickly farmers wash away their soil or the world's potash mines, the source of a conventional soil amendment, run out.

Though Sapsucker is certainly accruing benefits in the form of improved land and soil quality, these benefits aren't easy to turn into cash without selling the land. The reduced need for fertilizers and pesticides results in cost-savings, but that doesn't bring more money in the door. If anything, according to what Ricardo says, Sapsucker is at a disadvantage to farmers who can produce things more cheaply and so undercut their price. So how do farmers monetize stewardship?

It's not the actual environmental benefits that reward Jim and Debbie in the short-term, but the perceived ones. In other words, the story of Sapsucker and their land stewardship is a beacon for consumers who are willing to pay extra for environmentally friendly food. When that narrative is effectively communicated, it allows Debbie and Jim to raise the farm's prices above those their commodity competitors charge while remaining confident consumers will continue to buy.

The problem is, as Hannah, Georgie, and so many others have discovered, there is a ceiling to what a consumer is willing to pay when a cheap alternative is available.

Looking at Sapsucker's farm store, it's clear that controlling prices is a priority. Their six-month CSA is priced at less than $400, a reasonable figure for hundreds of pounds of farm fresh organic produce, eggs, and a kicker of hard cider (Sapsucker Farms, n.d.). In fact, they charge the equivalent of about $15 per week, which is competitive with average grocery store prices for the same collection of produce (Roos 2020). Their award-winning cider is the same. Though craft cider prices per ounce can vary widely, a local liquor store is selling twenty-two ounce bottles (the equivalent of about two regular cans) of Yellow Belly for $7.49, which is similarly priced to many ciders at my local grocery store (Haskell's The Wine People!, n.d.).

Though Sapsucker is certainly not trying to compete with bargain shopping prices, they aren't only catering to the most elite food buyers either. Their products are priced competitively enough to be available in mainstream retail locations. Though Debbie and Jim have certainly gained the "lifestyle benefits" of having a more livable property, rather than one that's being repeatedly tilled or sprayed with chemicals, it's hard to argue that healthy soil or clean water has been the source of their financial stability.

OCCAM'S FARM

My final guess, and eventual conclusion, as to Jim and Debbie's success was that a much more obvious factor was the source of the farm's stability.

In a word, wealth is the essential pre-condition that made Sapsucker possible and helped it thrive.

In many ways the wealth Jim and Debbie accumulated from their first careers facilitated Sapsucker's success. First, they were able to buy nearly two hundred acres outright. They acquired it while they were working other jobs and could afford to own it even as just a private wilderness for their own enjoyment, without agricultural tax exemptions. That level of wealth and security is no small feat for most beginning farms to achieve, especially given that Debbie and Jim didn't have access to a federal payment program. In fact, beyond the cost-share that supported the native prairie, the only regular federal benefits Sapsucker receives is an annual organic certification cost-share payment, which pays out $750 a year.

Second, as the farm grew and cider became a viable option that could support an on-farm tasting room, they were able to pay cash to construct the buildings and purchase necessary equipment. Not taking on debt to expand is a significant advantage that is out of reach for many new farmers who already carry relatively higher rates of debt than their established competitors (USDA NASS 2020a). These high levels of debt are also a significant threat to a beginning farm's long-term viability (Rabin 2010).

Third, Jim and Debbie also had access to significant intangibles. Debbie's background in marketing allowed her to evaluate farmers markets and understand they would not be a successful sales channel for farm products, so she never really wasted any time or energy pursuing them. Plus, as late-stage professionals just an hour outside a major metro area, Jim and Debbie were able to marshal considerable personal and community capital networks to establish their business and help it grow through the rough periods.

Finally, Debbie was financially secure enough to walk away from her job to start the farm's first product in part because Jim has continued on in his career as a pilot, providing an important financial backstop. That meant in the farm's early years the two didn't need to pay rent on the land or cover their personal living expenses through farm income. In other words, the farm didn't *need* to make any money at all.

Sapsucker Farms may be a good example of the kind of farm whose aesthetic we idealize and which we hope will continue to exist and grow far into the future, but the path Jim and Debbie walked is simply not accessible to most beginning farmers, or most Americans. Without significant existing wealth, and the skills and discipline to manage and grow it over time, Sapsucker would not be the farm it is today.

FARMING FROM THE BOTTOM

In some ways, however, Debbie and Jim's story is not so unusual. New farmers commonly start and sustain their businesses with either off-farm income (earned during or before starting the farm) or inherited wealth. Without access to one of those resources, many new farmers never make it.

"It's unsustainable in terms of living," Kate Dorsey told me by phone, reflecting on her career in farming so far. "You might have enough to pay your bills that month, but it's not going to really work in the long run."

Kate knew early in her life she wanted to spend her career farming, and the passion she has for the work is palpable in the earnest way she describes her experiences connecting with the land. But her grit and determination have not been enough to unseat the economic challenges of farming, even in the high-value "regenerative" marketplace.

Since graduating from college, Kate has spent all her free time and most of her professional time learning and working on farms. But after years of cycling through many low-paid jobs as a "farm intern" or "apprentice" gaining expertise as a regenerative farmer, she came to the conclusion it just wasn't working. So, Kate went back to the drawing board. Her conclusion? Find some other way to make money besides farming.

"I didn't see a way to become a farmer in a way I could feel good about without either having a whole lot more social capital or a whole lot more money," Kate told me. "Either you need to be able to network your way to a strong market for your personal brand, or you need to be able to eat the cost for a while until people know you exist." Kate knew from experience that many farms are heavily subsidized, or kept afloat entirely, by a spouse's off-farm job.

"I have yet to see someone actually make it work," she admitted, "in terms of getting enough income coming in that they can actually pay for expenses." This revelation was clearly unexpected and disappointing for Kate. Though farm work is her first love, and she wants to find a way to keep doing it, she decided the best way to achieve her farming dreams would be with support from off-farm income. So, she went back to school to become a midwife, a career which she hopes will allow her to pay a monthly mortgage on land and invest in perennial plants and other land improvements.

"I'm paying really for land access and access to some of the benefits that come with that, and I will pay for that with another job," she says. "I've already done that, right? I paid for farming opportunities. I've paid for access. I've paid to be trained. That's the foundation of farming right now. If you want to break into it as someone who doesn't have farming experience and doesn't have a farming family, you have to pay for it."

Years of knowledge and experience in regenerative farming practices weren't enough for Kate to find success, or even an opportunity to farm full-time. The same was true for many of the farmers she worked with.

It's telling that in our current discourse on the benefits of regenerative agriculture, it is often assumed that different practices alone are the panacea that will solve all the woes of agriculture. In this way, regenerative practices are not unlike the new-fangled technologies that have been "advancing" agriculture for decades. Tractors, crop protection chemicals, and genetically fine-tuned plants were also promised to be the difference-maker that would, finally, secure the prosperous fate of smallholder farming.

In my experience in the agriculture industry, I've seen that what happened to Kate and so many others is not a fluke or the result of unusual bad luck. Though the limitations of USDA data prevent us from gaining full clarity, some agricultural economists are still striving to understand this phenomenon. According to Dr. Mary Clare Ahearn's read of the data, farms don't tend to make money until they reach a certain scale, around twenty-five to thirty thousand dollars in annual sales, and average farms that achieve that level of sales also have well over half a million dollars in owned assets (Ahearn 2011). The evidence then suggests farming is a space where hustle is not enough; money alone ensures survival.

Reflecting on all the farms we've visited, poor and wealthy, old and young, big and small, this conclusion has surfaced again and again. It doesn't matter, really, what a farm produces, or where, who they serve or for how long, or how they treat the land or their communities. If a farm is wealthy, in the form of cash, income, or owned land, they're likely doing okay. If they aren't, they're dying. All the evidence points to the fact that a person really does have to be rich enough to farm.

Why, then, do we still cling to the idea that a lot of gumption and a strong work ethic are all a farmer needs to succeed? What maintains our strong, collective feeling that essentially anyone could farm as long as they want to badly enough?

Essentially, we've succumbed to the Yeoman Myth.

YEOMAN POISONING

This myth, as explored by Adam Calo (2020, 14), goes like this: Young, upstart farmers have, and will again, be drawn like moths to the flame of the "individualistic, heroic endeavor" of farming, to "create an alternative, more sustainable agricultural landscape." As Calo emphasizes, "This outcome occurs without having to reform the logics of the corporatized agricultural system" (21). In short, new farmers will save our broken system and overcome the sins of our forefarmers through sheer pluck alone.

This hopeful narrative is repeated again and again in the farming world. When it's pointed out that this story describes outcomes without detailing any plan as to how we get there, the answer always seems to be that young innovators will (through some undisclosed miracle-working) figure it out.

This kind of response makes it seem like farming is open to anyone and everyone who dares to dream. But anyone who's farmed, or tried to farm, knows it's not. As Calo (2020, 12) points out, the people who are able to make the investments and sacrifices necessary to even try to start a farm are overwhelmingly "educated, mobile, and second career or 'hobby' farmers." He describes the character of the American beginning farmer narrative as appealing "to a particular land use vision, one based on ideals of individual land ownership, single proprietor farming, neoliberal logics of change, and whiteness" (12).

What do we do then, if we want to support not just the already wealthy, privileged, and landed to become farmers, but anyone? Also, what will we do about the fact that the average age of the American farmer continues to climb, and we continue to be inundated with calls for new farmers?

Rather than asking, "How do we make more farmers," why aren't we asking, "What happened to the old ones?" (Calo 2020, 23).

We've accepted the fact of aging farmers as if there was some single, discrete catastrophe in the past that "wiped out" a whole generation—which there was not. The decline in farming over the last one hundred years has been continuous and was relatively consistent between 1935 and 1975 (Dimitri, Effland, and Conklin 2005). In other words, we've lost at least one generation of farmers (possibly more) because of the economics inherent to the current farm sector. Nothing about those conditions have changed in recent years, nor does the Yeoman Myth involve a strategy to change them.

"[I]n order to 'create' new farmers who will not quickly vanish or merely meet elite demand for organic foods," Calo (2020, 14) writes, "the *forces* that provoke loss of dignified and durable farming livelihoods must be identified and addressed." In other words, if we continue to motivate and recruit new farmers into the current system, we're doing little more than luring them into shark-infested waters.

One of these forces is undoubtedly land ownership versus land rent. For farms like Sapsucker, a key element of their success was owning their ground. Conversely, for farmers like Chris and Hannah, renting land is a weight on their businesses so great it eventually and inevitably becomes hard to bear.

The failure of beginning farmers to afford land rents is often blamed on the low price of food, laying guilt at the feet of consumers. But the Yeoman Myth offers a new lens through which to think about land rents. Calo (2020, 22) writes, "[beginning farmers] are perhaps better understood as vulnerable tenants." According to the 2017 Census of Ag, at least thirty percent of beginning farmers rented at least part of the land they used to operate their farm business, and competition, and thus prices, can be steep (USDA NASS 2020a).

Within this system, landlords have significant power to set and negotiate rental rates, which means in many cases they determine what kind of agriculture is practiced on their land. If landlords want to extract maximum rents, they are motivated to find a farmer practiced in maximum extraction (likely commodity grains or cattle). If they have a personal environmental bent, maybe they'll seek a more conservation-minded operator who might get a modest rent discount as acknowledgment of the added land-value benefits of their chosen practices. Especially among absentee landlords however, who are more likely to encounter their farm in a spreadsheet than on the ground, maximizing returns while minimizing risks are rational priorities. Comparing the risks and return potential of a new, inexperienced farmer versus a farmer like J.N. or a Clay, it's obvious why beginning farmers find it so hard even to rent farmland.

When the renting farmer is practicing sustainable or regenerative practices, which improve land quality and thus value, we see some fascinating economics take effect. If the essential assumption of for-profit businesses is true for farms, that the cost of producing a good is included in the price, then in the case of a new farmer using costly regenerative practices on rented land, they are actually asking their customers to cover the cost of both land rent and of *improving* the land. When the land isn't held by the farmer themselves, the landowner is collecting a double revenue stream, one in cash and one in increased land value over time.

Most of the time, the best a farmer-renter can do in this case is raise prices as high as possible so customers can help cover that double payment and endure the rest themselves. As we saw in Hannah's case, even high-income consumers are loath to pay the cost of improving wealthy landowners' private resources. Plus, there's nothing to stop a beginning farmer from spending years rehabbing rented land with regenerative practices only to have a landlord fail to renew their lease because now they can charge higher rents to a conventional operator due to the improved yield potential of the soil.

GOOD FARM LOST

Some might still be thinking that despite all the privilege Debbie and Jim had to accumulate to create Sapsucker Farms, it's still the aspirational ideal of a Good Farm.

If you're of that mindset, I'd ask you sit with the fact that this aspiration requires us to pin our hopes for the future of farming, and our food system, solely on wealthy heirs, heiresses, and second career back-to-the-landers. Almost every farmer we've met so far falls into one of these categories. For some, time and money are running out, or already have, as they inevitably do for farmers who don't have adequate wealth, land, and/or income, or who don't have ulterior motives that make farming worthwhile even when it costs them.[1]

It is clear to me that if Sapsucker Farms is the closest we can get to our Good Farm ideal, and their journey is held up as a path for others to follow, then the economic uniformity of America's farming community will remain unchanged. In doubling down on this dream, we are accepting the fact that the vast majority of farmers are elderly, already-wealthy men, and more than 98 percent are white.

---

1   An interesting, but thus far anecdotal, phenomenon I've witnessed: When ambitious new farmers get to the point in their farming careers where they realize there's no overcoming the fundamental economics of farming, they often turn to speaking, writing, teaching, and non-profit work. Beware of a farmer guru who seems to spend so much time on classes and book tours that they can't possibly be doing much farming. They may have transformed their business model, even if admitting that truth would undermine their whole value proposition as an expert.

If these are the only people who can achieve the Good Farm dream, what does that say about the dream itself? At the least, it says it's widely inaccessible and effectively a luxury of the wealthy—not unlike a yacht or private jet.

Where does that leave our desire to save and support Good Farms? From my perspective, we've tried to plot a course to this fantasy and found it impossible. We may have found farms that come close, but even those that appear to be Good Farms have fallen short in some meaningful way. In effect, after years of searching, I found no farms that truly met the spirit of the small family farm dream.

Beyond that, the pervasive assumption that most farms are Good Farms creates a lot of opportunities for the rich to get richer. From agricultural tax benefits to commodity payments and public donations to farm charities to sky-high farmer's market prices, there are dozens, if not hundreds, of ways the already-wealthy agricultural community has parlayed the Good Farm identity into even more money.

If this is indeed the case, I realized the reason I wasn't finding the Good Farms I was looking for was because I was asking the wrong question. Maybe it doesn't matter how well a farm fits our fantastical definition because maybe the definition itself is faulty.

It was time, I realized, to go back to the drawing board, to stop focusing on what we think a Good Farm is and start focusing on why farms are the way they are.

I mentally put each of the farms we've visited up on the wall and got out my red string. *What connects them?* I thought. *What is the common motivation that could be acting on all these farms and resulting in so many different outcomes?* Wealth and the desire to keep it was an obvious connector, but I sensed there was more to the farm wealth story.

If I could just find this common thread, I figured, maybe it would be possible to pull it, puckering the very fabric of what it means to be an American farm. Maybe doing so would allow us to bring together the community-feeding focus of Sapsucker, the longevity of the Mills farm, the economic viability of Clay's operation, the heart and determination Robert embodies, and the environmental ethic of Chris's farm into a single, viable blueprint. There had to be a common denominator.

Sapsucker's story held the key.

THE ROOT OF ALL FARM WEALTH

Besides wealth, another factor provided Debbie and Jim a significant advantage—one which is rarely recognized for what it is. Namely labor, specifically the unpaid variety.

According to Debbie, growing the Sapsucker team alongside the business has not been a challenge because the community has been helpful in filling in gaps during the farm's high-labor periods.

"A number of the things we do are actually like family activities, like maple syruping. People want to get outside and play, so they come up here, they help us put the taps out, collect the sap and make the syrup. It's kind of a community event." Though a few on-staff employees are involved with the cidery, the farm meets a significant amount of its labor needs by way of donated time and energy. Some labor is also compensated through in-kind support, such as the farm's World Wide Opportunities on Organic Farms (WWOOF) volunteers, who receive room and board in lieu of cash pay for a half-day of work. Ostensibly, WWOOF is an educational and cultural exchange program where volunteers get organic farming experience, and the farmer gains insights about the industry from the volunteers (WWOOF USA, n.d.).

Organic, sustainable, and regenerative agriculture practices require a lot of time, attention, and brain power compared to conventional ones. For most farms, however, labor is already the most expensive line on their balance sheets. While organizing the community to do labor-intensive tasks like harvesting maple syrup or trading education and room and board for garden work is an admirable conversion of social capital to financial capital, it should at least be recognized for what it is: a donation to a for-profit business.

Sapsucker is not breaking new ground here; staffing farms with volunteers is something of a trend among new farms in particular. This is in part because low-income beginning farmers who want to farm using regenerative or sustainable practices often find it impossible to provide livable compensation for their workers. In fact, as several of our farmers have experienced, many hardly have the cash flow to compensate themselves.

There's a big difference, however, between a business owner and an employee not receiving sufficient income. Like any other small business, most of the benefits of growing a farm aren't realized in wages over the farm's life, but in the payout when the entrepreneur exits. Farmers, in particular those who own land, are building that equity, and though they might not see regular or consistent income, they are gaining wealth over the life of the business. Debbie is no stranger to this idea.

"I'm sure there will come a time," she told me, "when we're going to be tired of this and want to sell it, and we would sell it." Though this isn't the plan in the short-term, Debbie says she's confident that when they're ready to leave the farm they'll be able to sell not only the land but the business they've built on top of it, thereby recouping much of the time and energy investment they've made. None of that wealth, however, is likely to make its way down to employees or volunteers.

The complicated questions around farm income and farm worker compensation are not exclusive to beginning farmers, either. In fact, every farmer we've met so far has struggled with the challenge of paying the people who do the farm's work, those people without whom there would be no American farms at all.

CHAPTER 6

CHEAP FARMER

———

For my first job out of college, I moved from Washington, DC to Sacramento. I was hungry for adventure, so much so that I decided against finding long-term housing before I got there and decided instead to take part in the World Wide Opportunities on Organic Farms program, or WWOOF—the same program Sapsucker Farms uses to connect with volunteers.

A month or two before the move, I found a farm in Vacaville, California, about half an hour outside of Sacramento, and made an arrangement with the farmer. I agreed to exchange about four hours a day of farm work for food and lodging. I was starting remotely at my tech job a few days after my arrival, so I cleared with the farmer that I could do farm work in the mornings, evenings, and on weekends as long as I could get the middle part of each weekday day off. He agreed.

When I arrived, the farm was as charming and quaint as I could have imagined. It was home to a kind of agricultural diversity I wasn't familiar with having grown up on the harsh and dry Wyoming steppe. There was an orchard of peaches and other sultry stone fruits, goats, hogs, and laying hens, and a hearty acre or so of vegetables we would be harvesting for the Saturday farmers market. On my first morning, there was a hot air balloon festival outside the next town, and while we did chores bright colors filled the glowing sky. I thought, *wow, this is truly it, the Dream Farm.*

The cracks emerged slowly. Within the first few minutes of arriving, the farmer began showing me each task I would be responsible for during the month of my stay. I was overwhelmed by the sheer volume of work that would be taken on by me and my fellow WWOOFer. I didn't meet the second volunteer, Jean-Luc, until later when the farmer showed me where I would be staying. I knew the living quarters would be an RV, but I was not told the RV would be shared. I found out when I was headed toward the bed to set down my bag and a thirty-five-year-old Haitian man emerged from the bathroom in a towel. He was equally surprised to see me, a twenty-one-year-old white woman who, I would later find out, he was also not told to expect.

"Not back there," the farmer grumbled, "there." He pointed to the front of the RV where a thin mattress pad was slung between the driver and passenger seats. Later I learned there was no electricity in the RV, the bathroom inside was unusable (we used a Port-a-John in the yard instead), and the shower was actually just a garden hose stuck through a hole in the RV's wall. But this was the adventure I signed up for, I told myself, and I should be glad to have such an authentic experience.

The days were long: 5 a.m. wake ups, dressing as best I could under a thin blanket for privacy, working (despite our pre-arrangement on hours) for four or five hours in the morning, and then another three or four hours in the afternoon. We'd gotten a couple of tasty dinners, but breakfast each day was plain oatmeal and lunch was bologna on white bread. I'd learned a little about Jean-Luc, too; he was on an extended trip from Haiti, paid for by the Haitian government, to learn about organic farming. He spoke French and Haitian Creole and very little English, so I tried as often as I could to help him to understand what the farmer was saying.

On my third day, Jean-Luc and I were waiting for breakfast after morning chores when the farmer told us we'd need to muck out the chicken coop that day. Jean-Luc asked me what had been said, but partway through my effort to translate the message the farmer cut me off angrily.

"He'll never learn English that way," he scolded. Abashed, I tried to explain that this immersion-only style of English learning was not working for Jean-Luc, especially when it involved explanations of tasks that he was expected to complete. The farmer dismissed me, turning to Jean-Luc. "You've been here long enough to know," he admonished. Jean-Luc had been in America for four weeks.

By Saturday morning, I'd already worked more than forty-five hours on the farm that week. We woke up at four in the morning to harvest for the farmers market, and by 8 a.m. we had enough freshly picked produce to sell. A few minutes away in downtown Vacaville, we spent the day moving lettuce, radishes, carrots, and cartons of eggs across the table. By about two in the afternoon, we still had much of what we came with, but the farmer was happy. He'd made about $300.

The next morning, Sunday, was supposed to be our day off—after chores, of course. I went back to the RV after to collapse into bed, but while I lay exhausted on my mattress pad, Jean-Luc showered, put on some of his nicest clothes, and left. I watched him walk down the gravel drive, onto the dirt road, and out of sight.

"He goes to church on Sundays," the farmer told me later. I asked if it was possible to walk, given that we were a good eight or nine miles from town. "No, he walks about a mile out to the main road, and someone from the church picks him up there." The farmer explained that Jean-Luc asked him for a ride, at some point, "but I was clear, Sundays are my day off."

FORGOTTEN FARMERS

The role of under- or un-compensated farm labor is often overlooked or dismissed as a thing of the past on American farms, even when its continued existence is glaringly obvious. Whether it's farmers not paying themselves, their families contributing free labor "for fun," volunteers or interns exchanging work for "education," or farmers taking advantage of vulnerable populations, failing to fairly compensate for farm work is as much a staple of American farms as wealth. In fact, under- or un-compensated farm labor is integral to the maintenance of farm wealth.

Though the desire not to pay for labor hurts everyone involved in farming, workers who are not related to farm owners are the most vulnerable, and most often exploited, group on farms big and small, old and new.

In particular, small farms with high labor demands, like fresh produce operations and dairies, tend to be highly dependent on undocumented workers. This is in part because navigating the legal foreign farm worker visa program (called H-2A) is seen as cost prohibitive or is otherwise inaccessible to small farmers, so they hire whoever they can, often outside the formal employment market (Vaughn et al., 2019).

To their benefit, most small farms are exempt from the principal federal employment law for farmworkers (the Migrant and Seasonal Agricultural Worker Protection Act of 1983 (Farmworker Justice, n.d.). Nor are they subject to the same level of reporting or inspection as bigger operations (Moskowitz 2014). Even among the farms that do fall under federal labor enforcement, the agriculture sector is so notorious for violations we don't actually know the full scale of agricultural labor abuse (Costa et al., 2020).

The USDA estimates the total number of non-family workers employed on small farms in 2020 is about 55,000 out of a total of over one million US farmworkers (USDA NASS 2020b; USDA ERS 2020b). This group has some of the most limited legal protections of any group of workers in the country, and we know very little about them (Moskowitz, 2014).

Beyond small farm exemptions, farmworkers writ large are totally or partially excluded from many labor protections enjoyed by other workers, from overtime pay to access to unemployment and disability coverage (DOL WHD 2020; USDA ERS, n.d., "Requirements for"). In fact, farms in general are exempt from so many labor regulations, scholars study it as the phenomenon of "ag exceptionalism" (Luna 1999).

Perhaps most importantly, roughly half of agricultural workers in the US are undocumented migrants (USDA ERS 2020a). Whatever few protections are afforded farmworkers in general are largely out of reach for a population whose legal standing in the US is in question; because in order to be protected by a regulation, a worker must feel secure approaching authorities to have it enforced.

This labor exploitation is also a direct reason why many farms stay in business. Farmer reactions to proposals that increase protections for farmworkers reveal that many farmers believe any action that increases worker protections, and thus potentially increases labor costs, will inevitably bankrupt their farms (Post 2019).

NOTHING TO FEAR BUT FARMERS THEMSELVES

The founding of United Farm Workers in the 1960s marked a turning point in the fight to improve protections for the US's foreign-born farmworkers, who underpin most of American agriculture (UFW, n.d.). Farmers have been fighting back ever since, often seeing the improvement of farmworker conditions and protections as a direct assault on their ability to do business.

Chris Pawelski, for instance, is a New York onion farmer and an advocate against providing more labor protections for farmworkers in his state (we spoke by phone in 2020). He says changes like adding a mandatory day of rest for workers every seven days and requiring farms to pay overtime after sixty hours of work a week (notably, a stipulation still far below other sectors) disproportionally affect small farmers who will have a harder time absorbing higher costs.

Among his other issues are that the housing rules for farmworker housing are too onerous for small operators (they are simply that farmworker housing, which is often included as compensation, must be safe and livable [NYS DOH 2016]). He wants the state to pay for housing improvements on his private property, or to be exempted from the rules. He doesn't want to pay for disability insurance for his workers because he doesn't have it for himself. He also thinks paying for unemployment insurance will discourage his workers from going elsewhere to look for work when his operation ramps down for the season and he lays them off.

Obviously, these rationales are inadequate reason for denying farmworkers protections. Business owners in every other sector are expected to consider the needs of their workforce and comply with regulations already in place. Farmworkers are people, and we have, as a democratic nation, decided that workers are entitled to certain standards in the workplace. Undeniably, the historical reasons for excluding farmworkers from protections included racism and allowing that legacy to continue today is a tacit affirmation of that motivation (Perea 2011).

Chris's perspective is common, in part because farmers who feel they are price-takers must focus on reducing costs, and obstructing policies that treat workers with dignity is one way to keep costs low.

But this perspective belies the fact that farmers have agency. No authority tells farmers what to grow, how to sell it, or at what price. A farmer like Chris could switch crops or change their wholesale plan to increase their revenue. They could build a brand and market directly to consumers or develop dedicated restaurant clients. They could grow a larger variety of crops or add livestock. They could take their farm out of agricultural production altogether, turn it into pasture or forest and graze livestock, sell hunting rights, or enter into a conservation easement. They could sell the land and live off the money or get another job. They could farm in many different ways and pursue many different paths to market. Change is not necessarily cheap or easy, but entrepreneurs are generally not rewarded for doing what is cheap or easy.

Many of these farmers are trapped in bottom-line thinking. This outlook is not unique to agriculture, but it's particularly pervasive in any industry where the product is a commodity. Bottom-line thinking is the mindset in which it's assumed that there's little the business can do to increase the price of their products (the top line), so all they can do is reduce their expenses (the bottom line) to earn more money. What follows is an obsessive pursuit of efficiency and cost-cutting. Turning to machines and other technologies is usually the first step in this process, but where innovation cannot replace workers, the labor itself must become continually cheaper to protect the bottom line. In too many agricultural circles, the moral wrong of exploiting vulnerable populations is an inconvenient fact of doing business.

The prevalence of bottom-line thinking in agriculture is evident in the damning history of labor on US farms. Over the last four centuries, Europeans and then Americans had many different ethically bankrupt strategies for minimizing or eliminating the cost of labor on farm balance sheets. The first strategy was chattel slavery. Later iterations after slavery ended included sharecropping and use of children (your own or others) as laborers (PBS 2012; Schuman 2017).

Tenant farming, where farmers rent land, and sharecropping, where farmers compensate landlords with a portion of their annual production, were common practices immediately after slavery. They didn't fall out of fashion until well into the twentieth century when developments in farm equipment had effectively allowed landlords to evict tenants and farm the land themselves. In fact, there were nearly 2.9 million farms fully operated by tenant farmers or sharecroppers in the US in 1935 (USDA 1935). Today, only 147,000 such farms exist, and this 95 percent decline accounts for most of the total farms lost over that period (USDA NASS 2019b).

In other words, many of the farmers who have left the land in the last one hundred years did not fail or go bankrupt. Their landlords simply saw a chance to make more money by cutting out the tenant. This trend was also driven by government policy that paid farmland owners to take land out of production, which allowed fewer farmers to own and farm more land (Daniel 2013, 9). These policies, in addition to a history of racist discrimination at USDA and throughout the agricultural sector, continue to be incredibly destructive to Black sharecroppers and tenant farmers in particular (Reveal 2017; Daniel 2013).

By the middle of the twentieth century, the implementation of the Bracero Program formalized the importation of underpaid foreign laborers from Mexico. It allowed US farmers to pay far less than minimum wage to workers who had few legal protections, a condition one congressman at the time likened to "legalized slavery" (Bauer and Stewart 2013, 1). Edward R. Murrow's documentary *Harvest of Shame* publicly exposed US agriculture's exploitation of migrant Hispanic labor more than sixty years ago (Blair 2014). The formal Bracero Program has ended since then, but little else has changed for undocumented farmworkers.

MILKING THE SYSTEM

No industry captures the propensity for bottom-line thinking, and in turn, the dependence on an undocumented workforce like the US dairy sector. More than 80 percent of milk in the US comes from farms that rely largely on undocumented immigrants (Adcock, Anderson, and Rosson 2015). If you're wondering how an entire multi-billion-dollar industry that's distributed across the country manages to pull off this massive violation of US labor law, meet Max, a third-generation New York dairy farmer and self-described "kingpin" of farmworker trafficking.

Outside of Ithaca, New York, I found Max's farm at the end of a two-lane road, past woods and open fields, a farmhouse, and a silo. I pulled off in front of a cluster of buildings, houses, barns, and a farm office. I splashed down into the muddy parking lot in the pouring rain and knocked on the door and was greeted by a grinning man of about sixty. This was Max. He spoke to me on the record, but after conferring with farmworker advocates and legal advisors, I am using a pseudonym to protect the safety and privacy of undocumented people he employs.

Max farms about 2,500 acres of farmland along with his eight-hundred-plus milk cows. When he brought on his very first migrant workers from Central America in 2000, they came to his farm through a staffing service which passed through copies of their official documents. He found an attorney right away, hoping to get them on the path to a green card. But the lawyer knew immediately the documents were fake.

"She said 'the only legal path you have to get legal workers in this country is the H-2A program, and these are not H-2A workers.'" The dairy sector doesn't qualify for H-2A because the program is explicitly for temporary, seasonal work, not year-round jobs (US CIS 2021). But the lawyer instructed him to fill out their employment paperwork like the documents were real.

"I kind of became the kingpin around here for workers," he told me with a shrug. The workers he already had were enthusiastic about bringing friends and family members to the farm.

"They said, 'But it's gonna cost $1,000 to get them here.' That's not much more than a plane ticket. So, they ask, 'Can you lend us the money and take it out of their paycheck after they get here?'...That $1,000 goes to a *coyote*, who gets him across the border. And then they'll show up here...in the middle of the night, with blacked-out windows and whatever." Until about 2012, Max says, that was how his farm got new migrant workers, and how he helped other farms in the area do the same. But then, he says, things changed.

"It very quickly went from $1,000 to a *coyote* to $7,500 to a drug lord because they could see this opportunity. [They realized] 'there's a whole human trafficking thing we're missing here.' So, they took over the getting illegal workers into the country, and the price went up." Max tells me the story with a mix of exasperation and resignation, like a butcher simply describing how the sausage gets made.

"$1,500 gets wired to a number. You have no idea. Goodbye $1,500...[That] buys you three chances across the border." Max says his guys have always gotten over during the first three tries. "The next $500 goes to the American rancher, who must have a turnstile or something, and charges $500 to these workers to walk across his ranch. They do it twenty at a time. So that's the second payment."

"After that, it's typically, 'We're in Houston, wire another $1,000.' 'We're in Atlanta, wire another $1,500.' Pick a city anywhere, wire more. And this continues until you wire the last payment, and then you don't hear anything for a couple days. And then you get a phone call that says your man is standing at the corner of 3rd and 42nd in New York City, and usually it's in the middle of the night. Someone races four and a half hours down to New York City, looking for some poor guy standing on a corner with all of his belongings in

a trash bag. So far the last three guys we've gotten that way."
As this route to obtaining workers has gotten more expensive,
Max has moved away from it, instead offering his workers
$500 cash to recruit workers from other farms in the area.

Hiring undocumented workers has left Max conflicted.
He told me the story of a girl, the cousin of one of his
workers, who had asked Max for a job. Upon finding out
she was fourteen he categorically said no, but his workers
made a firm appeal. They explained that her father had
been murdered back home and her sick mother needed
her to earn money. They told him that if he didn't hire her,
she'd go instead to the apple camps around Lake Ontario,
where she'd be in vulnerable, isolated housing with almost
exclusively adult men. Max eventually relented and said the
girl ended up being a terrific asset to the farm, though she
was not given the opportunity to attend school. She ended
up marrying a local and starting a family. Now she's an
American citizen, and she and her husband both own their
own businesses.

I spoke to immigration attorney Beth Lyon at Cornell
University about the phenomenon of child farmworkers in
American agriculture. The federal government has accounted
for well over half a million children working on US farms,
with as many as 100,000 likely undocumented (US GAO
2018, 87–88). This number is inexact, in part because federal
survey-takers have specifically avoided collecting data on
minors under the age of fourteen (39–49), which is a problem
because there is no minimum age for when children can work
on farms with their parent's permission (Neff 2011). Max's
story exemplifies other reasons for the statistical murkiness,
that either farmers or crew bosses don't know the real ages
of their young workers or don't want to, and certainly have

an incentive not to share them accurately. They usually can avoid doing so because farmworkers remain one of the most understudied groups, especially as compared to how much time and attention is spent studying farm business owners (Arcury and Quandt 2009).

I wasn't able to speak to the workers on Max's farm, but I was able to hear from other former and current dairy workers, including Crispin Hernandez, who has been a leading voice in advocating for stronger protections for New York farmworkers. In our 2020 interview at his home, Crispin sat down with me over a Spanish-English language translation app to describe the three years he spent working on a dairy farm in the early twenty aughts, and the long-term damage the work did to his body. Crispin says he was fired when he attempted to organize workers on the farm where he worked. Since then, he has labored instead to bring together and advocate for farmworkers on the state level as an organizer at the Worker's Center of Central New York.

Crispin's essential message is that farmworkers simply want to be treated with the dignity and respect afforded to other workers. Farmworkers want to get paid overtime when they work more than forty hours a week. They want to be able to rest so they don't get hurt or over-exhausted doing highly physical tasks. They want to know they're safe on the job, and that if they get hurt, they won't be fired immediately and left crippled and penniless, thousands of miles from home.

I asked Crispin what he thinks of the kind of pushback I heard from farmers like Chris Pawelski. The clincher of his response, which holds with what we've learned about so many farms already, is "It's not because they can't afford [to pay overtime, etc.]. The reason is they don't want to pay."

Many farmers I've spoken to praise the efficiency of workers from Latin and Central America, as compared to their American counterparts. Maybe there would be enough local workers to staff dairy jobs, some farmers told me, but they certainly wouldn't do it as well, or work as hard, as undocumented workers. Naturally, this isn't purely a difference of work ethics. One reason undocumented workers are incentivized to outwork their American peers is that they are, largely, at the mercy of their employer. Their residency status, their homes, and their ability to make money and achieve whatever goals drove them to make a dangerous international journey are all dependent on ensuring the farmer who brought them there remains pleased with their efforts. American workers, on the other hand, have more protections and act like it.

The cost of working in American agriculture for migrants is high. They may have access to more money than they would in comparable jobs in their home countries, but to access these jobs they have to cross the border illegally, put themselves in mortal danger, and then live and work at the whim of a farmer who they can only hope is a good boss and manager. Farm work, especially in the dairy sector, is also one of the most dangerous jobs in the country, and horrific incidents of workers drowning in manure lagoons or being crushed by equipment occur annually (Craig 2017).

The labor problem for the dairy industry seems intractable. Farmers trying to make more money feel trapped between years of falling milk prices and calls for more spending on labor. Part of the fundamental issue is that even as commodity milk prices have stagnated or fallen, production has continued to climb (USDA NASS 2020e). These are self-reinforcing mechanisms—the lower the price, the more milk a farmer has to sell to earn the same revenue, so production keeps climbing, and oversupply has become endemic. This commodity milk spiral offers all the returns to maximum scale, efficiency, and low-cost production in a near perfect parallel to commodity grains (and there's federal dairy payment programs too).

If the fundamental problem in dairy is that the price of commodity milk is too low, why don't farmers sell milk some other way? A big part of the challenge in dairy is biology: cows have to be milked three times a day, and that milk needs to be transported, pasteurized, stored, and sold on a rapid and precise timeline, even if it's going to be turned into cheese, yogurt, or whey protein. The marketing challenges of a quickly deteriorating product are significant, and dairy farmers often turn to established agricultural cooperatives or other commodity price purchasers to get their milk sold.

Without membership in a co-op, farmers would be on their own to either find a direct buyer for their milk or to build an independent business to process and sell it. But most farmers don't get into dairy because they're excited about milk marketing or logistics. Dairy farmers want to work with cows, so they have a strong incentive to stick with the co-op model, stomach the low commodity prices, and get undocumented workers by whatever means necessary.

VEGETABLE STAND(OFF)

It's not just dairy that struggles with dependency on a vulnerable labor force. Many of the unprocessed foods we eat, including fruits and vegetables, are also tended to and harvested by a large, foreign-born labor force. Fruit and vegetable farmers hire workers seasonally, therefore qualifying for the H-2A program, but many producers will tell you the price of complying with the law is too high.

I met Tony Emmi in front of a building with his name on it. It was closed at the time—a roadside fruit and vegetable stand just north of Syracuse. It was March, and the start of the fruit season on his three hundred-acre farm was still a few weeks off. We shuffled into the adjacent packing house to talk, it was a mid-sized warehouse where, later that year, hundreds of thousands of pounds of fruits and vegetables would be collected, sorted, and packed for shipping. But in March the building was empty and dark, the fourteen- and sixteen-hour days of peak harvest still a twinkle in Tony's eye.

Upstairs in the office, Tony told me about his third-generation farm. All those acres, planted in fruit and vegetables that need to be hand-harvested, require a lot of labor. No machine is yet able to quickly and efficiently harvest the likes of strawberries or fresh tomatoes in a way that competes with human hands, and for years the Emmi Farm has struggled with finding the staff to do it. He wants to pay more, he says, but he can't afford to because he's not getting any more money for his products. "It's just impossible," he says.

One of the farm's biggest customers told him in 2020 that they would accept no price increases for produce, and in addition, that they would be limiting what they would buy from the farm for the third year in a row. Retailing produce directly at the farm stand, Tony says, helps the farm get a little better margin, but the retail business is not large scale enough to pay all the farmhands, mortgages, and input costs.

The need to keep food prices low is often cited as a reason why farmers "have no choice" but to hold down their labor costs to the lowest possible level. But recent studies have shown that increases in farmworker pay have very little impact on the final cost of food, in part because the fraction of the average food dollar that currently goes to farmworkers is so vanishingly small (about ten times less than the farmer's share [Rosenberg and Stucki 2021b]). In fact, one researcher found a 40 percent increase in farmworker wages would only cost each US consumer about $25 a year—meaning a tiny rise in grocery store prices could radically transform the lives of these workers (Costa and Martin 2020).

Tony doesn't worry about the price of food as much as he does about paying the slowly climbing cost of farm labor. He says that if labor gets much more expensive in New York, he plans to get out of the wholesale produce market first, and perhaps just have a few workers on hand to sell retail produce at the fruit stand. If farmworker pay or protections increase significantly, he'll just transition all the cropland to a less labor-intensive type of farming (like corn or soybeans) and stop vegetable production altogether. He's not at risk of losing the land, but rising labor costs may cause him to leave the fresh produce world behind.

MISTAKEN IDENTITY

Today, farmworkers are doing about two-thirds of all the work on America's commercial farms, while receiving only a quarter of the pay (Rosenberg and Stucki 2021b). That work today is characterized by low compensation, seasonality that leads to months of unemployment each year, and physical destructiveness with serious consequences for physical and mental health. That remains true even if farmworkers are hired by farmers who acknowledge their humanity, and many farmers don't.

"There are parts of the agriculture industry that are so hostile toward their own workforce—it's insane," Robert, the Southwest citrus grower, told me by phone. Many of his neighbors and farms like his hire undocumented workers. He relayed the story of a local grower, an immigrant himself, who grew up during the Bracero Program, who he says has no sympathy for his workers.

"In his mind, when he came to this country, conditions were miserable. And if he could make it through that, why should he make it easier for them?" Robert sees and hears other farmers who want to have their workers live in tents, instead of providing them permanent housing, while driving around in brand new pickup trucks, betraying again, that it's often not the case that farmers can't afford to treat workers better, but simply that they don't want to.

A labor deficit continues to dog fresh produce farmers, and racism within the sector is an unquestionable driver. From Robert's vantage point, that fact may prove to be the industry's Achilles heel; because without migrant farm workers, very little produce would be grown, harvested, or packed in the US. He believes Central and Latin American farmworkers are already contributing so much to American agriculture that they should be granted a path to citizenship for their efforts.

A vexing part of this conversation for Robert is that regular people have so many good feelings about farmers, and yet little sympathy for farm laborers. "American attitudes toward people who work on farms is the exact opposite of the way they feel about farmers. Every man and woman who works on a farm across this country is a farmer. If you have the skills to work the land, you're a farmer."

Robert watched one of the farm's current hired hands, who arrived in the US when he was eight years old, struggle through the process of becoming a citizen while working as a laborer in the US and farming in Mexico at the same time. Robert's godfather was an undocumented migrant farmer, too, and to him these two men are the very embodiment of the American farmer. "But we don't think about them that way. We think of that as an unskilled workforce of ignorant people who don't have enough of whatever it takes to find another job."

Despite the outsized contributions farmworkers make in farming, the plight of laborers is usually overlooked or ignored in public discourse, which often results in the bulk of our sympathies (and resources) falling to farmers instead. Ricardo Salvador of the Union of Concerned Scientists believes this is because when it comes to labor in farming, problematic ideas are everywhere.

"It is really difficult for most people to realize," he says, "that labor in agriculture is the story of exploitation." Even in his experience speaking with well-informed audiences, it seems to him that farm labor is a question that few think about critically. "Too many think it's the natural order of things, that migrant workers have a particular slot in the hierarchy, and it's perfectly fine for them to be compelled to work in the slaughter plants or dairy farms." Teasing out why that expectation exists, he says, requires Americans to examine not only our nation's history of dispossession and racism against Indigenous people, but also the indelible links between slavery and agriculture, which exists legally to this day in the form of un- or under-compensated labor on American prison farms (Rice 2019). American agriculture has yet to reckon with that past in a meaningful way, and until it does the sector will surely continue to struggle to find the workers it needs.

THE COST OF A HANDSHAKE BUSINESS

Reducing the cost of labor on the farm isn't confined to cutting wages. Labor is the costliest bottom-line expense on many balance sheets, not only because it tends to become more expensive over time (employees want raises), but also because it never goes away. Next to only taxes, it is the main recurrent expense that a farm business can never shake. Whenever possible, then, farmers usually prefer not to reduce the cost of labor, but to get rid of it altogether.

The history of farm equipment and technology is one of eliminating the need for farm labor. For good reason—farm labor was, and largely still is, pretty horrific, despite the rose-colored glasses through which many view "our grandparents farms." An insight into the labor required on smallholder farms in the Midwest in the early twentieth century: "The memory of that agony [of harvesting corn by hand] rippled down a lifetime: 'That was true hell. Although we wore cotton gloves and covered our forearms with sleeves torn from old sweaters, the husks still managed to cut and scrape until our hands and arms were raw and bleeding'" (Vietmeyer 2011, 11). This months-long manual corn harvest was often completed by children and teenagers. Big families on rural homesteads were essential to have enough able bodies to do the work of commodity grain farming. Today, that harvesting work is done by hundred thousand dollar combines, and other demanding tasks, like weeding and pest protection, are taken care of with chemicals and advanced crop genetics.

Commodity growers who replace labor with machines and technology have seemingly moved beyond depending on free or under-compensated labor. But a closer examination reveals how deep American agriculture's bias toward unpaid labor really runs. Because as any technologist will tell you, new technologies rarely eliminate *all* labor, and the labor that's required in high tech systems is often much more highly skilled.

So where are these white-collar farmworkers?

Professional skills are definitely needed in farming. Even on the smallest commodity farms, the range of skills required to keep a farm business operational include: accounting and bookkeeping, legal work, mechanics, agronomy, hydrology, purchasing, sales and marketing, IT, investor relations, equipment operation, logistics, and trucking. Yet, even relatively large, high tech, and high revenue farms like Clay's are still staffed by a tiny number of workers, often without particular specialization in more than one of these skills.

This "lean" staffing represents a failure to invest in skilled labor, and it tends to lead to bad outcomes for farms. Lee Gross saw this time and time again in his work in Minnesota.

Lee was a county extension agent for nearly twenty years, with the particular job of helping dairy farmers prepare financially for expansion. At the time, many dairymen in the area were looking to make the big leap forward into modern, advanced milking parlors with room for much larger herds.

Lee described a typical financial planning meeting with a farmer around their kitchen table. It wouldn't just be him and the farmer. Usually, he says, the farmer's lender, the contractor who'd be doing the building, and representatives from the equipment provider, feed company, and the milk buyer would also be at the table.

"As we talked about these proposed expansions," Lee told me, "it was very clear to me I was the only person at that kitchen table who had the farmer's best interest in mind, besides the farmer. Everybody else was there to get their piece of pie." Sitting around the table, Lee explains, the pitch sounds great. The family farm can expand from fifty to 250 cows, and the companies involved could achieve fives time more sales without the cost of acquiring a new customer. The banker adds a great loan to their portfolio that's fully secured by land. Equipment dealers get paid right away, cash up front, and the milk plant gets more milk without having to deal with a new vendor.

According to Lee, many of the farmers he worked with at the time had amassed around $500,000 worth of equity. The typical expansion had them put all that equity at risk as collateral for a loan. By the time they were done, they'd often have spent one million dollars on upgrades. Then comes the depreciation. A $100,000 building might add only $50,000 worth of value to their real estate. A new piece of milk storage equipment, purchased for $50,000, might only be worth $25,000 on the resale market. The list goes on. That instantaneous depreciation doesn't come out of the partner's cut, Lee explains; it's a loss straight to the farm balance sheet. The risk and the majority of the costs, he says, weren't to the companies who were encouraging the expansion, it was to the farmers.

From Lee's perspective, everybody wins around that table except the farm. Any factor that might cause the farm to suffer, from a disease outbreak to an unexpected spike in feed costs to the bottoming out of the milk market could easily leave the farmer unable to pay their debts, leaving as the only choices selling out or filing for bankruptcy. Lee saw it happen repeatedly. Farm families walking away from attempted expansions with nothing, trying to rebuild their financial lives in their twilight years.

Part of what Lee is describing here is highly unusual. In most other businesses, the people weighing expansion strategies with an entrepreneur would have been invested partners or employees, or at least objective third parties, rather than outside consultants with their own agendas. Their incentives would have been aligned to make recommendations that were in the best interest of the farm business, and to conservatively consider the farmer's inherent risk. Instead, the people around these tables were representatives of their own businesses, offering advice as a complimentary service. That is a sub-optimal solution at best, but a natural result of an industry-wide aversion to paying the people who do the farm's work.

It seems obvious that outside advisors, who are not being paid to act in the best interests of the farm, might offer imprudent advice. However, the farmer *did* have the resources, $500,000 in equity, that could have been leveraged to pay to hear the advice of a skilled accountant, financial manager, or risk assessor, who could have offered an impartial analysis, unmotivated by the possibility of a big sale. Not *wanting* to pay for that advice, and instead accepting the free version, naturally, comes with a cost.

These farmers sat down at a table of people with vested interests in agribusiness, and those interests seemingly got what was best for them at the farmer's expense. It can feel like a story of corporate greed taking advantage of a consumer, but it is *not* that. Farms are not consumers, they are businesses, and for farm businesses, who's on the team and the payroll matters.

Throughout the modern commodity sectors, this type of "trusted advisor" relationship is common (Faleide 2017). Corn and soybean farmers depend on their sales agronomists, who are often employed by a seed or chemical company, to make agronomic recommendations. Livestock producers often depend on the input of their feed salesmen to tell them what rations they should be giving to their animals. These relationships are helpful to farmers who are "going it alone," but in reality, depending on a salesperson for advice the leads to key purchasing decisions is a fundamental conflict of interest.

TREAT 'EM LIKE FAMILY

Abuse of farm labor is something we've come to associate with "corporate farms." But focusing only on the biggest farms lets the Vacaville farmer I worked for, and so many other small farm operations, off the hook. One reason these discussions are less common among small farms is because it's not always vulnerable migrant communities that these farms exploit. Often, it's the farmer and their families themselves.

Many of the farmers we've met in this book draw little or no salary from their farms, and even paid business and personal expenses through savings or off-farm income, despite working grueling hours, and some, like Chris and Hannah, without even building much equity.

Labor exploitation is rife among farm families too, including children, which often leads to horrific accidents, in part because family members usually have no labor protections at all when working in farm businesses (LII, n.d.). According to the National Children's Center for Rural and

Agricultural Health and Safety, an average of thirty-eight children are injured on farms every day, and every three days or so a child dies on an American farm (Smith 2014). When it comes to underage work in particular, farms are some of the most dangerous and unregulated work sites in the country.

Farmer life-partners, overwhelmingly women, are also ripe for exploitation, though this can be a harder phenomenon to parse, mainly because most families in America benefit from two incomes (Sullivan 2020). The problem arises when one partner's income regularly and extensively compensates for the other partner's "work-related" expenses. What does that mean in practice?

Take the example I hear most often; a man runs a farm while his wife works in town, say as a nurse or a teacher (anecdotally an extraordinarily common situation).[2] The farm doesn't make much money, and some years it actively loses money, meaning over time it might net around zero income. Though gains could still be being made in terms of tax benefits, deductions and exemptions don't result in income.

But families, especially families with children, need income to cover healthcare costs, to buy food and clothing, as well as to pay for utilities and transportation. Most farms

---

2   Do gender distinctions matter? Absolutely. The USDA does not collect data related to the sexual orientation of farm couples, but you can be damn sure that almost no one imagining a "small family farm" is picturing one headed by a same-sex couple or a partnership involving more than two individuals. Discrimination based on sexual identity has a long and problematic legacy in American agriculture, one that can no longer be overlooked.

depend on a member working off-farm to provide health insurance (USDA ERS 2019b). For those other expenses, too, many small farms lean heavily on a family member working away from the farm.

Plus, this off-farm member is often *also* expected to work on the farm, whether it's a farm wife teaching by day and playing farm bookkeeper by night, or a farm husband, waking up at 4 a.m. on Saturday mornings after a long week at the office to pack produce for the farmers market.

A farm in this situation, because it's not making any or enough money, is acting more like a hobby. That's not to say many small businesses don't start out losing money; they often do. But it's less common in other sectors for a business in a money-losing state to continue for years. This is in part because making money is paramount for most other businesses, but in agriculture, simply wanting to be a farmer often trumps income motivations.

An off farm-employed partner who bankrolls a farm operation may experience a type of exploitation. Especially if it's expected that they make enough money and benefits to take care of all the family's expenses, with only the *possibility* that their partner might contribute as well. And when on top of that, the non-farming partner is expected to work at the business in their "free time" for free; it's difficult to see why this would be a desirable economic situation for a family.

Perhaps this disconnect explains why, in a recent DTN/*Progressive Farmer*/Zogby poll, only a bare majority of women involved in farming, 50.1 percent, said they'd recommend farming or ranching to their children, versus 66 percent of men (Miller 2020). The number of women farmers still trails their male counterparts. Women represent just 38 percent of principal farm operators; thus they are more likely to be the partner working and supporting their family away from the farm (USDA NASS 2019a).

FARMWORKER REBRAND

Rather than depending on technology, migrant workers, industry advisors, or unpaid family members, the new trend among progressive small farms is to utilize low-paid internships, apprenticeships, and straight-up volunteerism, like naive, young WWOOFers. In my research, I've found a significant community of former farmworkers who have taken part in these opportunities, and many were familiar with what I saw in Vacaville.

Kate Dorsey had one such experience, though she was paid. The farm she accepted an offer from was operating just the way she wanted to farm—intensive, organic vegetable production integrated with livestock, including pigs and chickens. It was also an economically viable opportunity in her eyes, since they were offering $1,250 per month in wages, in addition to room and board. But she says it didn't occur to her to ask how many hours of work would be expected.

"I assumed they would be reasonable, and they weren't. They expected me to work six days a week, twelve-hour days. It was grueling." Her day started at 6 a.m. and continued with only a short break for lunch until nearly sundown. This wasn't a case of callous taskmasters, the farm owners themselves, along with a second "intern," were working the same hours, tag-teaming care of their children all the while. It only took a week or two for Kate to realize that this level of work was unsustainable, and she approached the couple about a pay raise or to negotiate fewer hours or more breaks. They told her if she couldn't do the whole job for the original wage, there was no place for her on the farm. So, she left, as did her coworker. It's worth noting that, even if it's assumed that Kate's room and board were worth $750 (which is high for the rural mid-Atlantic), she was still being asked to work for about $6.94/hour, below even the federal minimum wage.

In all her work, Kate has yet to find a farm able to provide both a living wage and good lifestyle to owners and workers. In her experience, people are either working at tiny scales and have full-time off-farm jobs, or they're putting in back-breaking amounts of work just to stay afloat. "Either you are slaves to what you're doing, or you found some other (non-farm) way to make it work financially," she explained.

Some of America's most darling and celebrated farms utilize similar practices. Apricot Lane Farms, the subject of a popular documentary and a glowing *LA Times* article, is noted to be a "small farm" (again, that's less than $350,000 in annual revenue) while having a "team" of sixty people, including many volunteers and investors (McCarthy 2019). Even Polyface Farms, which was featured in *The Omnivore's Dilemma* and is renowned worldwide for ethical farming practices like rotational grazing, utilizes full-time "interns," who make just $100 a month in addition to room and board (Polyface Farms 2021).

Accessing labor at incredibly low costs from volunteers and/or apprentices is just as much a subsidy for small farms as any direct payment or tax break. The enforcement around internship rules, like whether these positions provide quality skills, is non-existent, allowing small operations to rake in labor hours from enthusiastic aspiring farmers for pennies on the dollar.

BEHIND EVERY GREAT FARMER

I'll be the first to admit that I sometimes have more stubbornness than sense, and the week I spent on this farm in Vacaville is a great example. That same Sunday I watched Jean-Luc walk to church, I called a friend to tell her about the situation, about the work, the farmer and Jean-Luc, about trying to keep up with my paying job, and about the spiders that lived above my mattress, suspended between the seats of an ancient Winnebago. It wasn't until that conversation, when I heard my friend's pause, heard her say, "So you're leaving, right?" that it hit me that what was happening here wasn't just agrarian work ethic in action.

It was exploitation, plain and simple. I spent half an hour hemming, hawing, and making excuses, downplaying the severity, trying to convince myself, more than my friend, that everything was really fine, that it wasn't a big deal because I'm tough. I grew up on a farm. Work doesn't scare me. To her credit, she never budged. She just kept repeating what I'd said back to me until I heard it for what it was.

The next day, I found somewhere else to live. I came back to get my things, and found Jean-Luc in the RV, resting. I asked him whether or not he could leave. He said he could not. The Haitian group that had sent him would come in a few weeks and they'd review what he'd learned (which was very little; the farmer hadn't been operating for long and was still figuring many things out for himself) and then he would get to go home.

When I departed the farm and left him behind, I felt like a traitor.

The Vacaville farmer embodied the dark side of the agrarian ideal. He was selfish, he lacked the work ethic he expected from us, who notably, were not "his workers," but volunteers. He felt entitled to our labor and treated us harshly for making mistakes that should have been entirely expected of people with little experience. He found differences, linguistic or otherwise, that made him feel excluded completely unacceptable, but did not hesitate to use the power of exclusion on others. He didn't even have enough compassion to drive a religious man to church on Sunday.

Yet to hear him talk, he was the red-blooded, progressive, Earth-loving farmer of crunchy farmers market fantasies. He could talk a big game about the problems of pesticides, he had a sprawling community food vision for his few-dozen acre farm, and most importantly, perhaps, he looked the part—a plump, middle-aged white man in blue jeans and a plaid button-up, with dirt under his fingernails.

What he didn't mention in those "ask a farmer" conversations with people at the market was that he didn't use pesticides in his orchards because Jean-Luc and I spent time every day clearing and setting gopher traps. He didn't mention that owning his farm was only possible because his wife was working full-time as a hospital administrator and living in an RV herself (a vehicle that did at least have electricity and sewer) so her husband could live his expensive dream of being a farmer. What he didn't mention was that, behind his lovable farmer facade, was a Black man and two women, who's time and energy he was harvesting to give his customers those warm fuzzies of supporting his small family farm.

For years, I wrote off the Vacaville farmer as a bad apple. They were inevitable, right? It must have just been bad luck, I thought, that brought me to that farm. It took me much longer, and meeting hundreds more farmers and farm laborers, to realize this farmer was not, in reality, a deviant in the farming community. In many ways, his actions and expectations were not far out of the ordinary at all.

It seems to me that American agriculture's refusal to appropriately compensate farm labor is as fundamental a feature of farms as wealth. Some of the very wealth that underpins successful farms, it stands to reason, has been directly or indirectly gained because workers were under- or unpaid. Uncoincidentally, American farmers are overwhelmingly wealthy, while farmworkers are some of America's poorest people. Many farmers have gotten rich harvesting cheap labor from unprotected workers.

Even after knowing all of this, perhaps there's still a part of us that believes the exploitation of farm workers is not the responsibility of farmers, but an inescapable result of the system itself, one in which both farmers and workers are powerless to do anything but go along to get along. That raw farm products are often commodities, and bottom-line thinking is prevalent, isn't necessarily a farmer's fault, and one alone doesn't have the power to change it. The system is much easier to blame for our knottiest, most complex problems because none of us made the system, so its existence and faults are not our direct responsibility.

If it is the case that the system is responsible for the fact that American farms have and still do maintain a massive amount wealth while also failing to appropriately compensate farm labor, then we'll have to dig deeper still into our agricultural history to find when and where this system failure occurred. Perhaps the past holds the secret to understanding how the threads of wealth and labor exploitation became such integral, yet invisible, parts of the American family farm story.

CHAPTER 7

FUBAR

———

The history of American agriculture is vast and deep. Agriculture, especially as we move into the past, tends to intersect nearly every aspect of life in every part of the country. Needless to say, an exhaustive history of American agriculture is well outside the scope of this book, so I was left with a quandary. How do I follow the threads of wealth and labor exploitation into the past to understand where they begin? I wish I could say my prodigious skill as a researcher put me onto the right track, but in reality, I caught my first break through pure serendipity.

While I was visiting a Virginia farmer in 2019, he mentioned that his dad ran a farm history museum, right on the property. It was in a red, prefabricated building with a padlock on the door and a sign reading, "We're Open By Appointment or By Chance," and listed a number to call. I pressed my face against the glass to look inside, feeling like a kid at a toy store. Chance was in my favor that day as I bumped into the owner, a genial old man with a booming laugh, and he offered to take me inside.

After an exhaustive perusal of antique treasures like perfectly restored tractors and seed packets dating back decades, I spotted a bookshelf filled with dusty volumes. I poked at the covers of Agricultural Yearbooks, annual reports published by the USDA, the earliest dating back to the 1930s. My finger came to rest on the spine of a book that looked a little bit older than the others, with a faded green binding that read "The Farmer's Book" in gold print.

I took it down gently and turned it to read the cover, where the title announced:

HOW TO MAKE THE FARM PAY

Or,

THE FARMER'S BOOK of PRACTICAL INFORMATION

On

AGRICULTURE, STOCK RAISING, FRUIT CULTURE, SPECIAL CROPS, DOMESTIC ECONOMY & FAMILY MEDICINE

The publication date was 1868. I was dumbfounded, both by the age of this literary treasure I had cradled in my hands and by the topic it purported to cover.

It was surprising to read that just three years after the Civil War had ended, when America's most sturdy, hardy, fantastical farmers—the vaunted pioneers—were rushing to claim land in the West, anyone would need the help of a book to make a farm pay. Before that moment, I had unconsciously assumed hundreds of thousands of families and individuals would only flock to an agricultural life if they already knew how to make a farm pay, and more, if they were confident it would. But the very title of this book seemed to call that assumption into question.

Passing a hand gently over the text of the preface, I was shocked at how familiar some of its ideas sounded.

"...Improved machinery, the better understanding of the rotations of crops, and the applications of manures, and the improvements in the breeds of domestic animals, have all helped to raise Agriculture, from mere drudgery, to an important science," the author, Charles Dickerman (1868, iii) writes. "The great mass of farmers are still laboring under the disadvantages of a false ruinous system of agriculture, without knowing just how to better their position."

It went on like that for pages. Apart from the dated language and obsequious tone, the words felt like they could have been written in the last few years. How was it possible in almost two centuries, the conversations in agriculture around practices, knowledge, economics, and labor could have changed so little?

This book offered an important piece of guiding data. In 1868 it seems, farmers were already scrambling to purchase books in the hopes of learning, not to farm well or feed their communities, but to make farms lucrative. It seems the "rich enough to farm" paradigm, and its attendant wealth and low-cost labor systems, were already in place by this time. We'd have to look further back then, before the 1860s, to find the source.

Upon seeing my near fanatical interest in the book, the owner insisted I take it with me to save it from collecting dust. It was well past midnight when I got home, but I couldn't help pulling out the ancient book again. Though the opening chapter failed to mention directly that wealth and low-cost labor were critical to a farm's success, I did find another clue in those onion-skin pages. The final passage of the first chapter was telling:

"[Progressive Agricultural Literature] has attracted the interest and awakened the kindliest sympathies of the wealthy and educated classes. Men who, by their energy and foresight, have

*acquired property or position, who once saw little in the hard
realities of farm life but drudgery and mechanical routine,
and looked with pity upon the farmer as one compelled to toil
without intellectual culture...have been led...to find in farming
ample scope for the highest intellect, and problems worthy of
the greatest efforts of human genius. This kindly sympathy
has elevated the farmer in the social scale, given his occupation the character and dignity of an intellectual pursuit, and
introduced him to a common brotherhood with men of culture,
science, and social position"* (Dickerman 1868, 28).

This gracious word-curtsey to the rich and famous who
had taken an interest in agriculture, got me thinking about
other "wealthy and educated" men in American history who
were elevating the farmer identity and giving agriculture the
"dignity of an intellectual pursuit." With a nod from Dickerman, I had my next lead, a gentlemen farmer who surely
saw himself as a person tackling "problems worthy of the
greatest efforts of human genius:" Thomas Jefferson himself.

AT THE TOP OF A FARMING MOUNTAIN

The grounds of the Jefferson estate outside of Charlottesville,
Virginia were verdant and smelling of lavender and ever-
greens on the cool and drizzly August day when I arrived.
Walking the wooded path to the great house, I couldn't help
but imagine how miserable it would have been at the end of
a long workday on the far-flung farm to have to climb the
hill Jefferson dubbed with the Italian for "little mountain,"
Monticello.

Coming out of the woods, I was first greeted by a mess
of unkempt vineyards, then a long vegetable garden, both

pressed off to the side of the main lawn in front of the residence. For all of Jefferson's big ideas about self-sufficiency and the pride of farming, he didn't seem much interested in actually looking at it. Farming to feed himself and his family, of course, was slave work on the Jefferson plantation.

After learning about many of the largely experimental plants Jefferson kept and studied from the plaques in the garden, I turned up at the main house. The tour I went on revolved almost exclusively around the rooms and treasures of the house. While stories of Jefferson's travels and exploits abounded, stories of Jefferson's time as a farmer were thin on the ground, even though we were standing on his farm.

Cornering the guide afterwards, I asked him, a retired historian from the University of Virginia, what the farm operation at Monticello was like in Jefferson's time.

"Most of the farming at Monticello, besides the botany garden and the failed vineyard, happened pretty far from the main estate," he began, haltingly. I sensed that the guide knew approximately as much about the agriculture going on at Jefferson's farm as our lauded forefather himself: very little.

"Frankly," he continued, "Jefferson was bored by farming. He was much more interested in new species, in horticulture and botany, and the science and discovery of it. He wasn't one to be very involved with the tobacco and cotton that were grown on the hills. Also remember, at the time of his death, despite owning about 5,000 acres of farmland and this mansion, he was more than $100,000 in debt."

These were interesting tidbits, especially given that Jefferson himself wrote in a letter in 1795 saying, "I am entirely a farmer, body and soul, never scarcely admitting a sentiment on any other subject" (Thomas Jefferson Monticello, n.d.).

Now, as then I suppose, it's great to be a gentleman farmer. Claiming the vaunted yoke of laborer, but without any of the labor.

In *"Most Blessed of the Patriarchs,"* Annette Gordon-Reed and Peter S. Onuf (2016) dig deeper into the agricultural paradox in Jefferson's life. Though born on a plantation and heir to two, Jefferson did not find the success he was looking for as a farmer, particularly as one who had to manage enslaved labor. One of his hallmark efforts to improve operations at Monticello, to "achieve the clocklike regularity of a machine," was thwarted by human beings who could not be threatened or bribed into acting as farm implements, rather than people. Three years after this attempt, Jefferson admitted defeat, writing that he was "not fit to be a farmer with the kind of labor" he had, namely, enslaved people (51). In other words, he blamed the failure of his grand scheme not on his own inexperience in farm management and his unwillingness to understand the limitations on the ground, but on the people actually doing all the work.

It seems, too, that Jefferson's love of his wealthy, gentleman planter life and his passion for the yeoman farmer ethos were not, in fact, one and the same. His records show the latter interest was part of a concerted effort to protect the former. He wrote in a letter to James Madison to the effect that the advancement of small landholding for landless whites would help soothe socioeconomic tensions that might, if left unaddressed, lead to the kind of unrest that would threaten large plantations like his own (Morgan 1972). Jefferson helped breathe life into the yeoman farmer myth, it would seem, not out of love of his countrymen and farming itself, but out of a self-preserving instinct to appease his poor neighbors with crumbs so they wouldn't flip over his banquet table.

Jefferson made many famous pronouncements on the benefits of small family farms in his effort to valorize the incredibly difficult and physically destructive work of small-holder farming. "Agriculture," he wrote in a 1787 letter, "is our wisest pursuit because it will in the end contribute most to real wealth, good morals [and] happiness" (National Archives: Founders Online, n.d.). The deep, intentional binding of agriculture to virtue and patriotism has been an ongoing American project and continues to this day. All the while, many have followed in Jefferson's true footsteps, by capturing massive land wealth, exploiting labor, and yet styling themselves as the small family farms that supposedly make up the backbone of America.

Today, Jefferson lives in our collective consciousness as the first and perhaps greatest advocate for the white, land-owning, yeoman farmer, but he did not invent the yeoman farmer idyll. The idea of independent families working the land predates even him. So where did it come from in the first place? This question is open to some debate, but it's instructive to begin at the point when small family farms first arrived in the Americas with European colonial-settlers.

WHATEVER FARM YOU CRAWLED OUT OF

When Europeans arrived on American shores, they brought with them, perhaps most importantly of all, the idea of private, alienable property. Prior to this moment, the system used to organize farmland ownership in America was grounded in Indigenous societal structures. These systems lasted not for five generations, or even sixteen, but for hundreds, possibly thousands.

The first Europeans to arrive in the Americas came seeking wealth (Zinn 1990). Though what they found in the Caribbean, Central America, and later, along the east coast of North America, were not the riches they sought in Asia, they found ample evidence of farming and of significant populations of particularly well-nourished people (Mann 2005, 40).

The idea that Europeans believed Indigenous Americans were hunters and gatherers living in a virgin wilderness is untrue. In reality, many of the earliest writings about Indigenous peoples note their advanced agricultural practices that were easily recognizable to Europeans as such (Hurt 1987, 27-41). The success of Indigenous agriculture is borne out not only in European historical writings, but in the fact that Indigenous people often provided food from surplus stocks to keep white settlers alive, and a huge amount of the world's diet today consists of foods pioneered by Indigenous agriculturalists (Mann 2005, 177).

To the best of our understanding, Indigenous communities prospered under a commons farming system—a true alternative to privately-owned farms. In this system, the community holds land and other resources collectively and controls and distributes them according to an individual's ability to use it (Hurt 1987, 65-68).

Though we are tempted to excuse Europeans their ignorance of this system, that would be dishonest. There was a pre-existing tradition of commons-style agriculture among European farmers, in England, France, and Spain (Greer 2012). In fact, the closure of common agricultural land all over Europe was fueling dramatic social change in the fourteenth and fifteenth centuries, leaving dispossessed Europeans with the choice of becoming tenant farmers, moving to an industrializing urban center, or immigrating overseas (McElroy 2012).

Nor is it correct to say Europeans settled only unclaimed wilderness. There was regular contact with nearby Indigenous groups from the moment of European arrival, and though communication was at times challenging, it was clear that effectively no land was "unclaimed" along the east coasts of the Americas (Mann 2005, 44). The fact that the land was actively being used for both hunting and cultivation was reason enough under European law to "grant" ownership to Indigenous people. In fact, in 1532 Francisco de Vitoria, a Spanish theology professor, said as much. He wrote that Indigenous people "were true owners, both from the public and private standpoint," of the lands they occupied and used. Pope Paul III further confirmed this perspective in 1537, saying Indigenous peoples should not be deprived their land or liberty (Hurt 1987, 77-80).

None of this, of course, stopped colonists from taking, by force or token purchase, Indigenous land. In this way, Euro-Americans became perpetrators of the same violence that was committed against them in Europe when the Enclosure Movement saw the landed elite dispossess peasants of commons which had been effectively managed, and which provided communities with food for generations. Many of these peasants arrived in America, saw the lands held in common by Indigenous people, and chose to expel and alienate them to pursue commercial agriculture instead (Hurt 1987, 75-76). They claimed common land as theirs alone to rule over absolutely, often without access to enough labor to care for it appropriately. This paucity necessitated another crime at odds with the democracy these settlers would eventually profess to love: chattel slavery.

This paradigm complicates the whole story of small family farming in the Americas. In this light, the patriotism embodied in the mythological yeoman farmer looks to be not simply about the virtue of feeding the country, it's more directly about taking the land, field by field, from Indigenous people. These farmers were Euro-American foot soldiers in the centuries-long war to dislocate America's original occupants. Why this led to our current, unrealistically elevated agricultural persona is clear: the Eden-like virtue of American farms was necessary to justify a genocide, committed to dispossess a continent's worth of land from thousands of individual groups of people with generations of prior claim.

Our modern, vague, and idyllic vision of farms as inherently virtuous, and all the exceptions that go along with it, papers over this legacy of European settler-colonialism with amber waves of grain-fueled cultural devotion. The agrarian-rooted American Dream told the world's downtrodden that they could come to this empty land and be free. But the land was not empty, and the promised freedom was predicated on the dispossession of Indigenous people and slavery. This agricultural freedom was always for the few, and for the rest, tyranny. This is the origin story—the past we perpetuate with our small family farm obsession today.

A COMMON TRAGEDY

In 1833, an economist would offer further justification for these actions, which is still very popular in anti-commons discourse today. British economist William Forester Lloyd wrote his famous essay that year on the Tragedy of the Commons (Hardin 1968).

His argument goes something like this: There's a small village of cattle farmers who graze their livestock in a big, open field, the common. The common is a wholly shared resource, which everyone has equal access to and which, because of its lack of ownership, is not governed by any rules. At first, everyone has one cow, and the cows graze on the common during the day and go home at night to the barn. But one day, a neighbor realizes he could get a second cow, and the common would be okay. So, he gets a second cow, and takes it off to the common with his first. But all his neighbors see, and suddenly the next day everyone has two cows. The grass gets cut a little shorter, but everything is still all right.

A while later, a different neighbor realizes if that neighbor could have an extra cow, why can't he have two extra cows? So, he gets a third, and goes to the common, and all his neighbors see, and suddenly they too realize they should get a third cow. Now the common is starting to look a little worse for wear. There's a lot of cow dung and not nearly as much grass. But there's more trouble brewing. Now every neighbor has suddenly realized the common is getting used up, it's going to be depleted eventually, and then there'll be nothing left. And if that's the case, I better get as many cows on the common as I can before anyone else does. That's surely what all my neighbors are thinking, and whatever I don't use is just going to be taken by somebody else.

The Tragedy of the Commons, in sum, is the idea that when a resource is held collectively, rational economic actors will inevitably arrive at the conclusion that whatever you don't use, someone else will, so you might as well use as much as you can, for as long as you can. This thinking inevitably destroys the common and lends credence to the argument that it's better for the sustainability of resources to "protect" them with private property rights because once they're owned, the incentives change. I don't have an incentive to entirely deplete my own resources when they could be sustainable, the thinking goes, because that would do me harm in the long term.

When I first studied economics, this theory was presented to me as justification for private property and for stealing American landscapes from Indigenous people. It was done for the good of the land and its resources—an act of compassion, of environmentalism. Farmers, this argument tells us, really are the original environmentalists.

What no one mentioned to me then is the Tragedy of the Commons has since been successfully challenged.

Enter Elinor Ostrom. Elinor was born in California during the Great Depression and through personal experiences, like planting a wartime victory garden, she gained an unusual reverence for the ideas of cooperation and resource conservation. She spoke many times in her career as a political economist about her early fascination with the idea that people in the common situation are "helplessly trapped into trying to get as much as they can for themselves" (Marginal Revolution University 2019). She was fascinated by it because she thought this idea was totally wrong.

Elinor went on to challenge the common consensus, in perspective as well as in practice, by eschewing the theoretical frameworks that were so central to economic theory at the time, which were the same as those that had led to the Tragedy of the Commons theory in the first place. Instead, she took the case study approach—paying close attention to how actual groups of people, in practice, who tackle these big questions about resources and community in real life.

"We found all sorts of patterns out there in the world," she said in a speech at the University of Indiana in 2010 (GBH Forum Network). "People self-organize common property institutions of a wide diversity of kinds, and sometimes solve problems very well."

Essentially, her work concluded, the Tragedy of the Commons contains a fatal flaw: it does not recognize "the possibility that resource users might hold property rights collectively and manage resources sustainably" (Poteete et al., 2010, 31). In other words, the assumption that people holding land in common can't or don't create rules and systems to protect the resource's integrity is a false one. Humans live in community and develop culture and society that can be stable and self-reinforcing. In other words, Elinor says, "Empirical work has shown that people have found ways of coming up with their own rules and extracting themselves from the problem" (Marginal Revolution University 2019).

In 2009, Elinor Ostrom became the first woman to win the Nobel Prize in Economics for her work in transforming our understanding of commonly held property. Her work gives us a window through which to understand and confirm that a farming system built around something other than private wealth and labor exploitation is possible.

The US's European founders made a choice to cordon off what was largely American commons for personal gain. In doing so, they committed immense violence to Indigenous peoples, to native species, to the landscape broadly, to the humans they kidnapped and enslaved, and inevitably to themselves and their communities, though a small number did manage to become fabulously rich in the process. Since then, we've spent hundreds of years justifying their efforts and lionizing their legacies.

For all these reasons, farming is inextricable from our ideas of private property, land ownership, and wealth accumulation. The reality is this agrarian system was as inconsistent with the goals of freedom and equality as it was with the American landscape. In attempting to build a democracy atop a farm economy predicated on stolen land and labor, our forefathers chose a foundation that had been cracked since the day it was poured. In the intervening years, many thinkers, including economists like Elinor, have worked to uncover and name this brokenness, despite post-facto justifications like the Tragedy of the Commons which have tried to rebrand the cracked foundation as a feature, rather than a bug.

All of this history helps us understand why the current paradigm, which separates "small family farms" from "big corporate farms," doesn't actually help us find the farms that work well because they're all just slightly different incarnations of the same dysfunctional idea. It's not the scale or the practice of farming that's broken, it's the whole idea we have of farms itself.

THE GREAT AMERICAN PIVOT

So, what do we do now that we know that the very roots of our farming system are buried in injustice and inequality, and that all our existing notions of what makes a Good Farm are similarly flawed? Nate Storey, for one, thinks it's time to think beyond small family farms.

Nate came by his small farm skepticism honestly. In the mid-2000s, he launched a startup on the premise that small family farms were inherently viable, if only they could access the right resources.

"Bright Agrotech was built on this theory that local ag is better for the world than super-distributed ag," Nate told me by phone in 2020, speaking of the agtech company he founded in Laramie, Wyoming, "and that small farmers—properly equipped, empowered, and educated—could actually be one of the catalysts for this local ag revolution."

Operating on that theory, he spent about three years at Bright scaling the business. But he came to realize that, given the rate they were onboarding farmers combined with the farm failure rate, it would take the company something like seventy years to have a meaningful impact on the food supply, and that was assuming continuous and exponential growth. That's when he started to question the premise on which he'd built his business. He realized that the belief that small farmers were mostly well-suited to being businesspeople was mistaken.

"Small farmers can be great farmers and bad businesspeople," he said, "but to have a lasting impact, they have to be both great farmers and great businesspeople, and that's just a really rare thing. And usually, the folks who are small farmers and great businesspeople end up being big farmers and great businesspeople." From his matter-of-fact tone, I got the impression that this was not the Earth-shaking realization for Nate that it was for me at the time. He looked beyond US agriculture for evidence to corroborate his suspicions, and he found it.

"We live in a country that has romanticized small family farms a great deal and has made the highest and best form of agriculture this small family farm. It's actually pretty unique to the United States. When you go across the rest of the world, people don't have the same kind of romantic notions." Nate guessed the reason for this is that Americans

are comparatively further removed from farming genera-
tionally, and we've collectively forgotten how miserable and
impoverishing farming can be. I disagree. I think it has more
to do with the fact farm owners have not, for some time
now, been the primary source of manual labor on American
farms, labor being the thing that makes farming miserable.
It's always been good to be a farm owner in America; it's
never been good to be a farmworker.

For Nate, realizing that the love of small family farming is
unique to the US prompted him to think about what, exactly,
Americans love so much about these farms.

"Yes, a farm that's close to the customer is able to deliver
fresher produce most of the time…[and] probably under-
stands that customer's needs better. But those aren't actually
things small family farms have monopolies on." In many
cases, Nate says, small family farms are not effectively filling these roles or offering the benefits for which they are
often celebrated. "I think the way to think about it is what
are the virtues of farming, either for people or for society, for cities and municipalities, for states and regions, or
countries? What does [or can] farming do that we value?"
When approached from that angle, Nate said, things start
to look different.

This interview marked one of the first times I was
prompted to think not about what we already profess to love
and treasure about farms, but about what we actually expect
a farm business to do, in their most essential form. After
some back and forth, Nate and I landed on three essential
functions for a truly good farm: produce healthy, affordable
food or fiber, create livable, stable jobs, and not contribute
to the degradation of soil, water, or other public resources.
These expectations aligned with those we might have for other

businesses; that they sell safe products, treat their employees fairly and with dignity, and that they don't damage the public trust while they do it. If these are the expectations, Nate points out, small family farms don't currently look like the best solution.

Since moving beyond Bright, Nate's acted on his realizations by joining Plenty, an indoor farming startup currently valued at over one billion dollars, as a cofounder and chief science officer (Sharespost, n.d.). From Nate's perspective, Plenty is a workable alternative to small family farms—a venture-backed company operated by a large team and powered by advanced technology.

The environmental failures of small family farms are a real concern for Nate, and he worries they are only going to become more exaggerated on the hotter, more crowded Earth of the future. He predicts the cost of farming's environmental impact will have to be priced into food eventually because governments simply can't afford to continue subsidizing agriculture by allowing farmers to damage the environment without consequences. Part of Plenty's particular value-add, Nate says, is that they're able to grow food near where consumers live and shop, and they do it without depopulating wildlands. Plenty's answer to J.N.'s "God isn't making more land" mantra is that maybe God isn't, but Silicon Valley can, and they can do it vertically, indoors.

Plenty is not, by far, the first group to imagine a farm system that doesn't revolve around private land ownership and low-cost labor. Alternatives have been around for centuries, since well before Europeans ever arrived on this continent. To find them, we'll have to confront our nation's agricultural history for what it is; an expensive and violent campaign to erase all but America's white family farms from the map.

We'll find these alternatives, then, when we recenter our agricultural conversation on the communities that have the truest claim to many long generations of farming on American land.

CHAPTER 8

BEFORE (AND BEYOND) THE SMALL FAMILY FARM

———

When I first talked to Randy Woodley, I asked if he was a farmer.

"Native people, we're not really good with categories," he replied, "it all kind of blends together. So, are we farmers? Okay. But we're not just farmers."

Randy's a gray-haired man with a kind face. He smiles easily. His agricultural journey with his partner, Edith, started in 1998 when Randy first had the vision for Eloheh (pronounced Ay-luh-hay), a Cherokee word meaning harmony, wholeness, abundance, and peace. They started searching for a place to bring the vision to life, and after four years, settled on a farm in Kentucky, in Randy's ancestral homeland.

"We bought fifty acres and a house and made it into a farm from scratch," he says, "and into a school and community." In addition to the farming school, the Woodley place was also an ecosystem of old heritage breed livestock, including Cherokee Choctaw mustangs, cattle, goats, heirloom seed plantings, and a sawmill and related businesses. There were about a dozen people living on the farm full-time at its peak.

"There's a lot of things you have to learn," Edith said of this farm community on the *Peacing it All Together* podcast in 2019 (3:39), "the do's and don'ts and how to work with other families and how to confront issues, and how to rejoice and have fun...But that's what we were doing." Randy describes it as a big success, everything they ever wanted. But then the realities of their slice of rural America set in. It started suddenly. One day they were living the dream, the next they were living in hell.

"All our neighbors came against us and decided they didn't want us to build a school there because we were Indians," Randy says (*Peacing It All Together* 2019, 8:29). He faced a barrage of racist attacks at a town meeting as his neighbors rose to demean his vision of a place for Native farmers to learn and grow. It was after that when the gunfire started.

"A white supremacist paramilitary group put up a .50 caliber submachine gun on our property line," Randy says, "and basically all times of the day and night began to fire it to threaten us." The local law enforcement officials would do nothing about it, Randy says, and they had no support. They were on their own.

For Randy and Edith, the safety of their children, their community, and the animals in their care had to come first, so they decided to sell the farm at a steep loss and move west to Oregon. Randy took a full-time job as a professor of faith and culture, and after years of uncertainty they were able to start again from scratch, settling on about ten acres of land in Yamhill, Oregon.

"Once we were chased off our land in Kentucky," Randy said, "I realized I'll never be able to live in my homeland again".

THE FIRST FARMERS

We're supposed to learn our history, in part, so we don't repeat it. Yet the history we learn, the story of "winning the West," of Europeans and Euro-American farmers finding an "untouched wilderness" inhabited by "noble savages," of the backwardness of Indigenous cultures that allowed white Europeans to dominate, is taught not just to avoid a hard look at the violent genocide in our history, but also to make it look like a necessary if unfortunate part of America's evolution. The impacts of that false history are still being felt, not just on farms like Randy's but across the food system.

The real history of farming in America begins with Indigenous farmers, whom Europeans knew from first contact were not cavemen-like hunters and gathers without agricultural know-how. We know they knew because the historical record is full of European observations of Indigenous agriculture (Mann 2005, 39–50). Hundreds, if not thousands, of unique Indigenous groups and cultures existed across the Americas by the time of European contact, and farming methods developed in the more populous Mesoamerican region quickly spread across the continents (19–21).

To create and sustain these many and complex societies, Indigenous groups maintained many property and land tenure systems. Though these systems were likely not vague, our knowledge of them is incomplete due to the concerted effort by Europeans and Euro-Americans to wipe out Indigenous history and cultures (Hurt 1987, 65). Despite the dearth of information, researchers have identified some broad similarities among some of these groups:

"Tribal property was much like corporate property: every village member was a landowner, but he or she did not have absolute control of the land. An individual could not sell it, and among certain people, an individual could lose his right to the land if he left it untended. If an individual cultivated the land, however, he or she could do so indefinitely without interference from any other person" (Hurt 1987, 74).

In other words, cultivated and uncultivated land was held by the community, and within that land, individuals would be granted enough to grow what they needed to support their family. When cultivated land became exhausted, the community could move on and resettle elsewhere within the uncultivated land they controlled. Though only a small part of a group's territory was regularly in intensive farm use, much of it was used extensively in proto-agricultural systems which alter landscapes to improve hunting, fishing, and gathering—for example, utilizing planned burning to create meadows which lured deer into the open for easier hunting. Almost universally, Indigenous peoples did not have a conception of immutable and alienable individual property rights (Hurt 1987, 66). Instead, they managed land commons collectively.

For all the modern claims that this kind of system was unwelcome among Europeans, the rash of people who abandoned settler-colonial villages to join Indigenous society suggests otherwise. Perhaps it was the more equal role of women in Indigenous culture, or Indigenous people's freedom to express individual liberty (Johansen 1983, 17–19). Or maybe these escapees were drawn by what Jefferson himself believed was a more "egalitarian distribution of property" which "secured for Indians in general a greater degree of happiness" than the poor in European-style governments (103). Whatever the reason, many aspects of Indigenous cultures seemed to have been down right alluring to their European neighbors, and according to Benjamin Franklin, many could not be convinced to return to Euro-American society after parting from it (National Archive: Founders Online, n.d.).

For our purposes, the most important difference between Indigenous and European societies is how they organized food production. Indigenous farmers, for example, overcame the limitations of labor quite elegantly. In many groups, individual control of farmland was derived from an individual's ability to use it (Hurt 1987, 68). This concept was not foreign to Europeans, who had their own principle of "use ownership," or squatters rights (66). This system allowed every family the space needed to feed itself, while preventing the accumulation of land beyond one's ability to put it to use. It also meant a newcomer to the community wouldn't need to have pre-existing wealth to join the farming class; as long as they could do the work, the land was theirs to use. Compared to our modern farming system, which is incredibly exclusionary, limited to those with existing wealth, and ruled by the instinct to hoard land whether or not it can be put to good use and farm it whether or not it leads to good economic or environmental outcomes, this system is a breath of fresh air.

It's worth noting that there was no universal system of land ownership common across Indigenous nations (Hurt 1987, 65). Different climates, peoples, geographies, and circumstances led to many unique sets of institutions; some patriarchal, some matriarchal, some nomadic, but many sedentary. To Randy's point, Indigenous people are farmers, but they are not just farmers, and just as paradoxically, each band and clan similarly defied being collectively described by any overarching generalization.

Though modern arguments have claimed that, in general, a lack of private property would curtail productivity or hamper technological advances, the evidence in Indigenous history suggests otherwise. Most Indigenous communities were skilled in farming and proto-agriculture, using these practices to create food and fiber surpluses that supported large, stable populations, with excess to use for trade (Mann 2005, 129–132). Today, the global food system is heavily influenced by Indigenous crops, which have defined global palates for centuries. The ubiquity of maize, or corn, for example, is a telling illustration of Indigenous farmers' technological prowess. Scientists today remain uncertain how Indigenous cultivators were able to breed ancient teosinte to produce modern maize, meaning ancient Indigenous farmers understood something about plant breeding that even modern scientists can't uncover (18).

Smallholder agricultural life for colonists, as compared to nearby Indigenous people, was incredibly hard. European farming styles were not well-suited to American climates, were relatively non-diverse, and left colonists with recurring "starving times" as food stores ran out (Cochrane 1981, 20–21). It provided some food, grueling work, and relatively poor environmental outcomes as compared to

Indigenous abundance and practices that sustained agricultural production for centuries. This makes sense when it's considered that most early colonists were not farmers to begin with and did not plan to be for long. Farming among early Euro-Americans was not motivated by subsistence as much as by the "get rich quick" schemes of selling high value tobacco paired with land speculation, or the belief that land in the developing colonies would one day be much more valuable (14).

It is clear, then, that if what we want from farms is good food, good jobs, and good environmental outcomes, obliterating Indigenous food production models and murdering and erasing their practitioners was the original sin. By and large, that choice has been repeated, again and again, for centuries, right through to today.

STILL FARMING

"I grew up in a community that is considered subsistence farming. I hate the term 'subsistence,' but people understand what that means," A-dae Romero-Briones told me by phone. She's a Cochiti Puebloan and Kiowa Indian, and the director of programs at the First Nations Development Institute. "Most of the people in my community were farmers, and my grandpa was a farmer, and so we grew up in a Pueblo community doing Indigenous agriculture, which we'd been doing for thousands and thousands of years." Over the last few hundred years, A-dae says, racist intervention by the US government have led to the devastation of her people's agricultural tradition. For her tribe in particular, an Army Corp of Engineers dam project threatened to flood a significant amount of their agricultural land. She remembers being a small child watching the tribal council and the wider community struggle with an existential question.

"'Who are we if we're not farmers?'" She said, describing those long-ago conversations, "and the answer was, we would absolutely not exist." The tribal council ended up taking the US government to court. Since that moment, A-dae knew she would spend her life being an advocate for Indigenous farmers, or planters, as she describes them. The case may have ended, but the cultural war against Indigenous people's way of life has not.

"The 'assimilation' of American Indians has not stopped," A-dae says, a startling matter-of-factness in her voice, "We still are consistently challenged, about how we grow, collect, and produce food." This is particularly galling from A-dae's perspective because Indigenous land management practices have provided so many of the uncredited insights that define the permaculture and regenerative movements today (Lundahl 2021, 111–112). Stealing the ideas of Indigenous tending, A-dae warns, and applying them as if they were discovered by white farmers is inevitably flawed because the practices are empty, and will eventually go awry, without the stories, culture, and heritage behind them.

From A-dae's perspective, the fundamental missing piece of modern American agriculture is this human element. She began to understand this while she was studying economics at Princeton, hearing the words used to talk and think about growing food that are borrowed from capitalism.

"The language we use to talk about these systems is always about relationships between inanimate objects, theories like price and value, or practices and soil, or nutrients and diet. It never, ever acknowledges many of these cycles begin with the intentions of humans, the community or the person."

The language of modern farming, A-dae says, betrays the false assumption that human decisions aren't elements of the system. But of course, they are. Without humans, farming doesn't exist. The problems in the current system aren't in the relationship between price and value or between the soil and water, A-dae says, it's the relationship between the people in the system we keep getting wrong, between landowners and workers, between food producers and eaters, between growers and sellers. All of these people and relationships, she says, cannot be understood in isolation.

The way A-dae talked about these relationships reminded me starkly of Randy's unwillingness to categorize or be categorized. And this same resistance to definition existed in A-dae's perspective on land, too.

"There's still this idea that farming and agriculture happens in a square," A-dae says, bringing to mind the view out the window of an airplane. "But really, that's still missing the point. Because everything outside of that square will affect that square, but we rarely ever talk about what's outside of that square." In other words, she says, nature does not recognize or respect private property. It operates on the scale of watersheds, ecosystems, and so, necessarily, on the level of community, not the individual or family. Assuming decisions made on one acre can stand independent from those made on each of its neighbors' is simply another iteration of the flawed understanding that a part can be separate from the whole system.

"In America," A'dae continues, "there's such an individualistic idea about success that's embodied in every sector, from agriculture to business. You're assessed, and your success is attributed almost exclusively to individuals. And that's really damaging to systems that require communities, like agriculture." For Indigenous people, she says, particularly when it comes to farming, it's all about community. In her Pueblo community, for example, everyone in the community has a role in farming. "One of the elders described it to me as like a dance. There may be one person dancing, but outside of the circle all of the community is watching. They offer a dancer water or a place to sit when they're resting. There's a role for everybody in agriculture." But the dominant US farming tradition, she says, relies on a model where the farmer grows the food, and the consumer goes to the farmers market or the grocery store to buy it, and there's no mutual support. To A-dae, this is not a sign of independence, but a sign of being isolated and vulnerable.

Despite the fact that private land ownership and exploitation of labor have been defining characteristics of US agriculture, Indigenous farming traditions of the past and the present stand as monuments to the fact that there have always been alternatives. Today, the Gila River and Yakama people both collectively own and operate extensive farming operations (Gila River Farm 2021; Confederated Tribes and Bands of the Yakama Nation 2021), and one of the largest irrigated farms in the country is owned and operated collectively by the Navajo people (Navajo Agricultural Products 2021).

Other communities, particularly religious minorities, also farm in a distinctly more communal tradition. The Hutterites in Montana and the Dakotas have become farming powerhouses, providing well-priced, high-value, quality crops (Ogletree 2018). Their farms are operated communally (Riley and Stewart 1966).

(UN)COMMON POWER

Following in Indigenous footsteps, other marginalized peoples have refined their own communal farming traditions in the US, finding strength not in smallholder farming pride and independence but in pooling resources to advance the common good.

When Europeans forcibly brought enslaved Africans to America, it represented the first arrival of highly skilled farmers from across the sea. It is not an exaggeration to say that for generations many white property owners in America knew little to nothing about farming, and their livelihood depended entirely on the skill and knowledge of African farmers (Carney 1993). There are some rare cases where this truth comes out in the historical record. For example, a Southern peach planter noted in 1901, "I went South with the idea that the negro was a rather stupid creature," he began, only to correct himself to name Black farmers, "the best agricultural labor in America to-day...way ahead of our New England Yankee" (Okie 2016, 100). This farmer's acknowledgment of Black farmers' prodigious skill did not, of course, mean he paid those who worked for him more than a quarter of what a white worker would earn (102).

In the midst of this violence and compulsion, expertise and erasure, collective farming in the Black community arose and perpetuated (White 2018, 5–8). In Monica M. White's seminal work *Freedom Farmers* (2018) she explores how, from the very earliest moments of arrival, Black communities in America have used food and farming in the commons style both as a way to survive and as a form of resistance (8–9). Her research identifies several examples throughout history where the establishment of commons and collective work were used as a viable alternative to small, independent family farming businesses, which were nearly as far out of reach to Black farmers in the Jim Crow South and thereafter as they were during the times of slavery.

The earliest examples of this work, after the "impressive range of independent production and marketing activities" of enslaved Africans in the Americas, are embodied in organizations like The Colored Farmers National Alliance and Cooperative Union, or Colored Farmers Alliance (CFA) (Barickman 1994, 649–687). In 1886, CFA had more than a million members across the country who "exhibited collective agency by pooling their resources to purchase land and tools and to offer loans for black farmworkers" (White 2018). Each chapter of CFA was self-governing, and knowledge and information was actively shared between chapters. Members were collaborators, rather than competitors, mutually invested in each other's success (14–16). Variations of CFA and its successors continue right through to today, where organizations like the Federation of Southern Cooperatives keep the national, collaborative tradition alive.

CFA aimed to help people born into slavery not only acquire and hold land, but to farm well, both for subsistence and for profit, the latter being essential given that many Black farmers were tenants or sharecroppers. The high rate of non-ownership among Black farmers was no accident—in the Jim Crow South, Black farmers had little access to credit, and racist policies at the federal, state, and local level contributed greatly to Black farmers never accessing or losing land (PBS News Hour 2019). These realities meant the work of CFA and similar organizations was not only about empowering the disadvantaged but was also about fighting back against a system that was trying to eliminate Black farmers altogether.

By the 1960s, civil rights and Black Power organizations were recognizing "the importance of land ownership, of supporting rural black farmers, and the critical role of southern agriculture in feeding urban populations of African Americans" (White 2018, 17). In 1969, Fannie Lou Hamer started the Freedom Farms Cooperate (FFC) in Sunflower County, Mississippi. With just 680 acres of land, FFC grew to host nearly a dozen distinct businesses and missions, from a community garden to low-income housing for African Americans in need, especially those who had been evicted or fired for voting. FFC took in former sharecroppers and tenant farmers and provided educational opportunities, among other forms of assistance (White 2017, 1).

Other Black farming collectives followed. The North Bolivar County Farm Cooperative acted on a regional level in Mississippi to "improve the diets of many of the poor families in northern Bolivar County," one of the poorest in America in the 1950s and '60s. By 1968, the collaborative group of farmers produced more than one million pounds of food, including "sweet and Irish potatoes, a variety of greens, snap and butter beans, black-eyed peas, and cantaloupes" (White 2018, 92). This co-op would go on to not only make strides in feeding the community and paying its farmers decent wages, but also in growing successful food businesses as well.

Though not all these initiatives endured—often for reasons outside their actual viability, namely systemic racism—these stories of Black farming power embody the resilience of the communal farming systems in the face of extreme economic and social hardship. The lessons learned by Black communities across the American South indicate variations on commons-style farming can develop even in the most unfriendly of circumstances and can be put to use to feed communities and empower (and pay) skilled farmers. These are powerful truths to uncover in a world where anything other than a private property-based farming system is beyond the ability of many to imagine.

Where Black communities have found commons-style farming systems useful for flexing and shifting through long periods of systematic discrimination and injustice, other communities have found similar benefits in different places.

TRIAL BY FARM

In the American West, the Chinese-American and Japanese-American communities have a history of collective farming. In states like California, people of Asian ancestry have played an outsized role in agricultural production for centuries. Valerie J. Matsumoto explores just such a collection of Japanese-American farm communities in her book *Farming the Home Place*.

First, its necessary to understand the many racist impediments to putting down farming roots that Asians and Asian-Americans have endured in the recent past. California's Alien Land Law of 1913 prevented people of Asian ancestry from purchasing land or leasing it for more than three years, making it almost impossible for nearly two-thirds of the state's farm laborers to acquire land wealth (Matsumoto 1993, 25). Racist furor fueled this legislation, and one of the widely known motivations for passing this restriction was a fear of competition from Asian farmers among white landholders (46).

One Japanese-American farm system that came into existence around this moment was the brainchild of Abiko Kyutaro, who established three agricultural communities in an effort to offer Japanese farmers a place to settle (Matsumoto 1993, 25–26). With the passage of the 1913 law, many residents in Abiko's communities could no longer legally buy or own land themselves, but were able to circumvent the law by purchasing land in the names of their American-born children (31).Over the next few years, as World War I veterans returned, anti-Asian sentiment flared in California, so much so that in 1920 in Merced County, California the local Farm Bureau directors "formed a special committee of delegates from fraternal organizations and boards of trade" to become the Merced County Anti-Japanese Association (31–32).

Merced County was home to Abiko's third and final community, Cortez Colony, where thirty Japanese American families persisted despite the discrimination they faced. The land they'd purchased was harsh desert, and it took years of intensive management to coax it into producing valuable stone fruits, grapes, and nuts that are common there now. In the face of severe anti-Asian sentiment, the community founded a cooperative to both purchase inputs and sell the food they harvested. The Cortez Growers Association (CGA) helped the individual growers overcome the challenge of doing business across a language barrier by working as a collective. Along with local churches and civil organizations, Matsumoto credits the CGA as the glue that held Cortez together, economically and socially, when American racism tried to wipe their community off the map (Matsumoto 1993, 54).

In the aftermath of Pearl Harbor, Japanese Americans across the US, but especially on the West Coast, experienced a raft of indignities and assaults on their rights, from curfews and travel restrictions to "evacuation" and internment in concentration camps. The farmers at Cortez were forced to live in the Merced Assembly Center for several months in 1942 before being relocated to Granada Relocation Camp (Amache) in Colorado. At this time, thousands of Japanese farmers lost farm leases, and thousands more were forced to sell homes and farms due to the uncertainty of their return. In the words of one historian, the Japanese diaspora in the West was "virtually eliminated" by this displacement (Matsumoto 1993, 99–100).

It was the collectivized nature of Cortez and the other two Abiko farming communities that allowed them to endure. "The people of these colonies negotiated a unique economic arrangement that provided for the supervision of all their farms during their absence," Matsumoto (1993, 100–101) writes. Doing so allowed them to maintain ownership of their property and ensure they'd have a farm to come back to after the war. In a race against internment, CGA leaders met and devised a custodial program for their farms. The organization they assembled identified a board of trustees, an advisory board, and a tough white farm manager to oversee operations on all the farms and arranged for advisors to come to Colorado annually to review farm operations with each of the owners.

At the end of the war, anti-Japanese sentiment continued, due in part to the fact that the businesses and farms Japanese-Americans had been forced to vacate were productive and profitable, and the usually white tenants who were operating them in their absence didn't want to give them up (Matsumoto 1993, 153). Threats and eventually terrorist violence became common throughout the rural West as wartime opportunists tried to discourage the return of Japanese-Americans to their homes (154–155). But the people of Cortez returned to their farms anyway, often living in tents on their own property while waiting out the annual leases that had been signed on their farms. In these times, too, the people of Cortez lived communally, and this tradition would persist through the 1950s and 1960s. Between the many established mutual aid channels and civil organizations that existed, the farms at the colony, though individually owned, often acted as a collective (156).

The story of Cortez Colony reveals the unique ability of collective farming systems to survive dramatic disruption and to adjust quickly to changing circumstance. Knowing this is critical as we look to the uncertain future of American farming, one that's increasingly likely to face frequent social, economic, and environmental disruptions.

The experience of Asian-American farmers in the West, as well as Black farmers in the South, also offers another, deeper insight. Namely, that white smallholder farmers have been granted special treatment and advantages over other groups, in labor and land markets, and in the eyes of the law, for centuries—and where has that gotten us? Despite four hundred years of granting extraordinary privilege and an endless series of "hand ups, not hand-outs" to America's small family farms, we are still being asked to provide more and more financial support, exceptions, and social power to this group all the time, while all the promised outcomes remain just out of reach. If disadvantaging alternative farm models with the likes of Jim Crow and the Alien Land Act was not enough of a head start to make small family farms truly viable, it begs the question of whether *anything* could bring the Good Farm to life.

While much of America's white voting public remained engrossed in the Euro-American Good Farm daydream, communities of color were dealing with America's farming reality and carrying on the legacy of a true, and much more functional and resilient, alternative.

The long history of communal and collectivized farming in the US, capable of withstanding decades of hardship as well as extreme shorter-term circumstances, offers real hope for an alternative to the vehement, self-defeating independence of the small family farm idyll. Young organizations are reaching into these histories to structure new ventures in old ways.

FARMER RECLAMATION

One such organization is The Abundant Table, a farm in Southern California. I met its interim executive director Reyna Ortega via Zoom, speaking in lyrical Spanish and sitting next to her fellow farmer, Linda Quiquivix, who goes by Quiqui (key-key). Reyna was formerly a manual laborer in the conventional fruit and vegetable sector; now she's a part-manager of the farm. That's because on May 1, 2020, The Abundant Table decided to make a transition from non-profit farm focused on ethical land management, worker dignity, and serving low-income communities to a worker-managed farm collective, pursuing those same goals.

A key driver of the transformation was the organization grappling with whether the farm should be self-sustaining and be building wealth for its workers, or whether it should focus on its non-profit work and aim for bigger goals in the future. There was deep disagreement, and some workers left as a result of the final decision, but in the end, those who stayed did so because they were committed not only to farming, but to doing the racial justice, equity, and food access work their non-profit status allowed. Making a large monetary profit for members, they collectively decided, was not their top priority. Since their decision was finalized, it's been a whole new world at The Abundant Table.

"We recognize all voices are important," Reyna explains, "and we decided under what conditions we work in a more democratic way." The new structure empowered its members to participate, and the cooperative as an entity was very much built from the ground up by its members.

Quiqui, who also acts as translator, never wanted anything to do with agriculture, in part because the roles available for People of Color in modern agriculture are almost exclusively limited to demanding and low-paid manual labor. But after a long personal journey, she found The Abundant Table, and had no idea she was joining the organization at such a revolutionary moment-- when the workers in the organization were renegotiating their role in the farm's overall decision-making process. She says the amazing thing about the reorganization is that the fundamental power shift didn't destroy the farm; the organization was able to change without everything falling apart.

Today the cooperative meets as an assembly regularly, with Reyna as the spokesperson for the workers. Though each member only has to do forty hours of work per week, they often end up spending time sitting on committees, working with the board, and participating in the management and decision making of the organization. Extra profit, after living wages are paid, goes back into the work of providing free and reduced-price food boxes to low-income, Indigenous communities. They strive to grow food that is culturally and ecologically relevant. In addition to growing melons, peppers, and tomatoes—all traditional Mesomerican foods—they've started growing carnations for Day of the Dead celebrations as well as ancient *papalo, verdolaga,* or common purslane, and *quelites.*

"One of our foundational principles," Reyna says, "is to provide low-income and low-access communities with really healthy organic food. We used to provide that through the schools, but the school system changed and wasn't ordering from us anymore. We asked ourselves what are we going to do? Can we just forget that part and just continue with the revenue producing stuff?" The answer was an emphatic "No." Instead the group went back to the drawing board and created low-cost food boxes. "There's always going to be a challenge, but as a collective and with the broader community, we can give each other the ability to maneuver through these changing realities and challenges, like a pandemic," she says with a chuckle. "We don't say 'sorry, there's nothing we can do.' We figure it out, collectively."

A farm managed entirely by former farmworkers is, in itself, a radical departure from our modern conception of farming, but the boundary-busting doesn't stop there. The Abundant Table is also majority woman-owned and led. Reyna believes this diverse leadership in farming is only natural.

"Tending land, farming, is always an invitation to honor all of our femininity, which is not gender-based. It's an invitation to do the deep work of nurturing, tending, caring, and the life that comes from that is the life we're a part of, we're co-creating that...and so being able to hold the power of the feminine in the work we do and honoring the feminine of the land, in contrast with the overly masculine, domination energy of the industrial agricultural around us, puts a big mirror up to the need for that feminine energy in our industrial food system. And we could, no matter how we gender identify, be open to that invitation to honor the feminine in the work we do in agriculture." In other words, farmers who seek to embody the virtues of nurturing, care, and tending should have a special place in agriculture, regardless of gender.

One of the biggest existential challenges for The Abundant Table has been that it doesn't own its own land, and the land they're currently farming is accessed only through a lease that expires every few years.

"We don't have anything stable or secure to put our feet on," Reyna says, "and every year we say, 'We survived this year, we're still here.' And it's been that way every single year for the last ten years." Finding a more secure land base is essential, but incredibly challenging in an impossibly expensive Southern California land market.

Having a land base, where the members can settle, control the price of their own housing, and learn the unique ecology of a place that will be permanently theirs, is still a goal that's far in the future for The Abundant Table. They continue to strive for it, in part because, for these farmers, the land is very much part of the team.

A telling illustration of how that ethic works: Early in 2020, before the farm declared its collective intent, all the organization's hopes and dreams rested on one acre of strawberries. Strawberries are an expensive and desirable fruit, but they're also hard on the land and extraordinarily sensitive. The growers were thinking of these strawberries as their golden ticket, their lottery winnings that would help them escape the hard spot they'd fallen into. But the strawberries were struck by a blight of spider mites, and the whole crop was critically damaged.

"Just listening to what the land was telling us," Reyna says, "what we heard was the strawberries are dying in the old institution, signaling the old way of thinking of The Abundant Table also needed to die. I told my partner, 'Oh shit, we're screwed. Over. Done.' But he said, 'No, no, I'm going to just keep sprinkling beneficial spiders to eat the spider mites. I'll save them. I'll save them.' Eventually he stopped because it wasn't working, and we learned sometimes we have to be open to that. Sometimes relations come to their end. Death isn't always physical." They learned their lesson, and they waded into the collective endeavor despite their fears.

In the end, the strawberries came back.

THE OLD WAY FORWARD

After the move to Oregon, Randy and Edith resurrected Eloheh and are still striving to realize their vision for a community for Native and non-Native farmers and tenders to learn and grow.

"I know there's no such thing as a small sustainable farm," Randy tells me, while Edith cans green beans somewhere out of sight. "If that's your goal, that's gonna be really difficult...You can't really sustain yourself from a small farm." That's why, he says, he doesn't primarily consider himself a farmer, but a host for people interested in learning about a different worldview.

After arriving in Oregon, Randy and Edith tried to recreate what they had in Kentucky with limited space and without being able to offer room for other families to live on the property with them. Still, a community came together around the farm, of both Native and non-Native people, and Randy and Edith were able to plant hundreds of fruit-bearing trees and bushes as well as inheriting a successful Indigenous seed business with locally adapted fruit, vegetable, and herb seeds.

The vision Randy has for Eloheh is not one of a giant food empire that takes on the current ag system. Chris Newman—the farmer from Virginia—on the other hand *is* aiming for that goal. A couple years ago Chris moved his farm, Sylvanaqua, from Charlottesville further East to the Virginia tidewater region. He has a different outlook these days that clashes gloriously with the beginners' optimism he shared the morning we first met.

"After a while," Chris said in an interview, "the engineer in me just could not help but do the math around the amount of food that needed to be produced, and the amount of food that [the food] movement was producing. We quickly realized there was a lot of virtue signaling going on in the regenerative ag movement. We weren't operating at the scale that we needed to. We were still operating under some not-so-great assumptions around farming oriented around nuclear families and oriented around command-and-control ownership and retaining that owner-worker divide that tends to be fairly exploitative" (Investing in Regenerative Food and Ag 2020, 3:11).

Today, Chris says, he's not worried about the "small family farm" lifestyle. He's looking to scale and integrate the farm into a complete, and profitable, direct-to-consumer food business. "We're busting up the whole family farm paradigm because there's just a lot of problems with it," he says (Investing in Regenerative Food and Ag 2020, 4:19).

One of those problems, Chris says, is small family farms simply can't compete. The idea that the small yeoman farmer could go toe-to-toe with ultra-modern farm and food businesses relies on the idea that they'll be competitive in the aggregate, that no individual small farm could take on Big Ag or Big Food, but thousands and thousands of small family farms, running diversified operations, might be able to.

"If those farms were going to replicate like that," Chris said, "it would have happened already. But they haven't because it's too difficult to make a living as a farmer doing that. There's very little historical precedent for that kind of farming to actually work without creating some kind of exploitative relationship with the people who are doing [the work]" (Investing in Regenerative Food and Ag 2020, 6:20). As we've seen, he is right.

Sylvanaqua Farms, with whom I now work, is aiming to operate at a much bigger scale and under a different model. Rather than relying on a single farmer-owner, Chris is spinning up a farm collective to ensure the people he works with can receive fair compensation and have a meaningful stake in deciding how the operation is run. His experience has made him deeply suspicious of farms, however idyllic their story or beautiful their social media accounts, that don't rely on appropriately compensated work.

~~SMALL FAMILY~~ BIG TEAM FARMS

The evidence of a strong tradition of collective farming that has succeeded socially and economically in America, particularly as organized by communities of color, is incredibly hopeful. These stories suggest it's not too late to change the way we grow food in this country. Independent family farms have overwhelmingly proved themselves incapable of meeting the challenges of the past, let alone those of a hotter, dryer, and much less certain future. But collective-farm alternatives offer a blueprint to something fundamentally different, not a small family farm, but a big team farm.

The big team farms we've seen have provided evidence that they do a better job meeting the three good farm goals; providing satisfactory jobs for workers and owners, healthy, affordable, appropriate food for customers and communities, and good environmental outcomes that preserve the quality of land. These farms follow in the footsteps of Indigenous peoples of the Americas, of Fannie Lou Hamer and the North Bolivar County Cooperative, of the Japanese-American farmers of Cortez Colony, and of the leaders of vertically integrated, collectively managed businesses the world over.

The old saying goes, "The best time to plant a tree was fifty years ago. The second-best time is now," and that saying resonates with the current problems in our food and farming system. If we had interrogated our obsession with the settler-colonial agrarian myth, and therefore our deep cultural, social, and political commitment to small family farms, fifty, one hundred, or four hundred years ago, we might have saved ourselves from a public health crisis driven by overabundant sugars derived from overproduced commodity grain (Fields 2004, 820–823), a fresh and saltwater pollution crisis across much of the United States (Kling et al., 2014), an aging and emptying countryside (Semuels 2016), and an ethnically and gender-homogenous class of farmers who own so much farmland it's nearly impossible to start farming without being a millionaire (Horst and Marion 2018).

It's time now to rethink our vision of what an ideal farm looks like. It's time to abandon our love of the agrarian aesthetic to prioritize good outcomes over charming, distressed wood and overalls.

The good news is millennials and Gen-Zers want to farm. They want to use their hands and do physical work; they want to participate in climate change mitigation and help feed their neighbors and communities. Young people of every stripe are anxious to farm, and it's time we talk about real solutions that allow them to do that. There will never be enough small family homesteads, nor will there be enough wealth to purchase them, or money to educate and inspire them to entrepreneurial self-sufficiency. There never was.

But big team farms offer an entirely different path, one where the technical skills of being a talented land tender can be fairly compensated, and where other skills, from marketing and logistics to accounting and people management, are also valued. Big team farms offer a path to repopulating the American countryside, building wealth for younger generations, restoring our degraded landscape, and transforming our food system for the good of public health.

What it takes is a real reckoning with private farmland ownership, and putting people, lots of people, big teams of people, back into the equation. This is good news for the next hundred years because if any part of the system has capacity for resilience, it's the people.

CONCLUSION

As we find our way forward, the problem we face is now one of transition. How do we get from the farms we have now to the ones we want?

To begin, we have to move beyond the popular idea that American agriculture is perpetually in crisis, and that existing farmers are an impoverished group in need of financial support. For example, remember Hannah's story from the opening of this book? Now that we know how rare it is for a farmer to be both low income and low wealth (as Hannah was) and a consumer to be relatively rich, we can understand Hannah's story for what it is—the exception that proves the rule. The takeaway then is that consumers do not hold ultimate responsibility for the failures of the farm system. When comparing the average consumer to the average farmer, the farmer is much more likely to be economically stable and able to afford a price change. When we begin a transparent conversation about expectations for farmers with the knowledge that they, as a group and also as individuals, are holders of vastly more wealth than most, we can start a fundamentally different discussion.

We also must contend with the fact that those who have suffered, and continue to suffer, the most at the hands of our agricultural system are not farm owners, but the generations of workers and other exploited and dispossessed people whose formidable contributions to feeding America are often cropped out of our agricultural picture. By reinforcing the "farmer as victim" narratives in our media and public discourse, we further erase these people and allow those who continue to benefit from the fruits of oppression, in the form of inherited wealth and privilege, to divert public resources from the truly disadvantaged.

The agricultural industry writ large has done little to correct this public confusion between farmers and farmworkers, and for good reason: It's much more profitable, socially, economically, and politically, to be seen as small, poor, subsistence farmers and not as multi-million-dollar companies owned and controlled by wealthy families. The "family farm" label makes the industry's calls for reducing or eliminating farm labor protections, environmental regulations, and taxes seem much less insidious. In the gap between our agrarian fantasy of family farms and the reality, many of our country's wealthiest and most powerful citizens—including politicians (Hayes 2020), business leaders (Shapiro 2021), and celebrities (Murdock 2018)—hide wealth and land they'd like to keep, but at a lower tax rate, and the bonus social capital that comes with being a farmer.

The perceived universal goodness of farmers also provides cover for practices that run counter to the public trust, and even when we're made aware of practices like excessive irrigation (Sanderson, Griggs, and Miller 2020), over-application of chemical fertilizers and pesticides (Wertz 2020), and confined raising of livestock (USDA NRCS, n.d.), we instinctually write them off as the work of "bad apples" despite the evidence that they are common.

We buy the "all farmers are good" story because we are primed to. We've been prepared our whole lives to side with and fight for the farmer underdog. It fits squarely into many of our preconceived ideas of not only agriculture, but of America, and has proven a powerful way to mobilize public opinion to defend the preferences and priorities of an almost exclusively wealthy class of people.

"Won't you help me," Old MacDonald from the song asks us, "after I raised you and all?" What we can't see is he's just a cardboard cut-out shielding people who, on average, are wealthier than 90 percent of their fellow Americans (USDA ERS 2020c; Urban Institute 2017).

Across journalism and policy realms, we often defer to farmers as the experts, and even in public discourse, the idea of "asking a farmer" any and all questions related to food and farming is prevalent. But those with a private profit motive have much to gain from selling a particular story, rather than unbiased truth, and therefore we should not accept farmers, or any other private business owners, as unquestioned authorities on their own work. The idea that farmers are the only people who can have knowledge or opinions about farming is just one of many conflicts of interest inherent in agricultural exceptionalism. If we hope to move beyond the current paradigms, we have to acknowledge farms for what they are, businesses, rather than altering our expectations in the hopes that doing so will help them become something more.

All this to say, thoughtful, intentional farmers are out there who deserve the goodwill we lavish on all farmers indiscriminately. But in general, the idea that "all farmers are good people" does much more to protect bad actors than those doing good. This is because when in the public eye, family farms, regardless of size, income, or practice, often claim the story: "I'm just a lowly family farmer trying to get by," which comes with sympathy and public support unique to this industry. In this way, we allow a vanishingly small number of exceptional farmers to provide cover for an entire industry.

The good news is, we now have the tools to challenge this overly simplistic routine. To such an extent, I'd argue, there's good reason to retire the "small family farm" label altogether and offer extreme skepticism to any who would use it to argue for benefits. The gap between what we believe small family farms to be and what they often are is simply too great. Allowing the label, and its associated narratives, to persist only encourages exploitation to continue.

The truth is the American Farmer story, in nearly all its incarnations, has always been more myth than reality. The problem is that somewhere along the way, we forgot that The Plucky Farmer is a parable and decided instead that it represented a blueprint for something real. Personally, it took me a long time to come to terms with the fact the legacy I hoped to inherit was little more than a fairy tale, falsely "proven" through carefully told, one-off stories (though of course, even a broken clock is right twice a day).

THE CLIMATE-FARM NEXUS

The amount of public resources that have been funneled to farmers in the form of land and money in the past four hundred years to pursue this myth is unfathomable, and yet somehow as fewer and fewer hands have hold of this wealth, the more they seem to demand.

The most recent incarnation of these demands is farmers seeking public and private financial rewards for transitioning to practices that might sequester carbon and help head off climate disaster (Abbott 2021). This seems extraordinarily disingenuous, given that most farmers already have the financial resources to make these investments, and that benefits of these practices already accrue to them in the form of improved productivity. We would find it unpalatable if other industries, especially well-capitalized ones that are active sources of environmental degradation, demanded governmental payments to pursue better outcomes. Instead, we regulate companies to force them to do better.

There seems to be no acknowledgment in these discussions that, as we've discussed, farmers already receive vast public benefits annually and have become quite wealthy because of them. If the American taxpayer is one of the main financial investors in so many American farms, then it is not incumbent upon the taxpayer to pay for farmers to contribute to the public good. We have already paid. Now is the time to put stipulations on federal payments, and if farmers don't want to change their practices to protect our public water, air, and soil resources, then they are free to forfeit their payments, tax exemptions, and other public benefits.

In the future, it will be a more prudent use of public funds to write environment regulations for agriculture, and actually enforce them, or to buy farmland outright from farmers, than to attempt to compensate them annually for climate mitigation. This strategy also avoids another inevitable outcome of paying farmers to grow commodities "more sustainably": namely, that it further incentivizes and entrenches the commodity grain production system. Giving more money to commodity grain farmers, in other words, has never led to less grain, which is what would truly be the best outcome for the planet.

None of this is to say that regenerative practices are not effective or fundamentally better for the health of people, soil, plants, animals, water, air, and the environment broadly. Evidence suggests that they are. But farmland owners already receive financial compensation for using regenerative practices in the form of long-term increased land value. The demand for additional, short term compensation, I think, could be easily and defensibly ignored.

Pretending like family farms simply need new, more "Earth-friendly" farming practices to reach the mythical place where prices and productivity balance out in favor of smaller, poorer, more ethical farms ignores the fact that nothing about these practices changes the fundamental economics in agriculture. The belief that paying for carbon sequestration will transform the farm sector is akin to building a new house on quicksand that has already gobbled up a dozen others—but believing this one will survive because it's made from a slightly different material.

Our endless fretting about agriculture's environmental impact seems woefully incomplete without consideration of agriculture's immense human injustices and inequities. The two problems are intrinsically linked and cannot be solved in isolation. Addressing the racist and fundamentally unjust treatment of farm labor would radically transform the way agriculture is practiced in the United States in a way that, by necessity, would be more environmentally friendly than our current system.

PREPARING FOR A RURAL RENAISSANCE

If there are no Good Farms, then it's worth asking how we should describe who is farming today. In short, farmers are just people. With all the hopes and doubts, fears and dreams, shame and successes of anyone else. Farmers aren't split into discrete moral categories; small, virtuous, hard-scrabble families and giant, corporate boogiemen. There are many, many shades of farm and farmer in between. It's not a brotherhood or a priesthood. It's a business sector. It's not an identity. It's an activity, one done by choice.

If we care about the future of our nation's food system, security, and environment, finding paths by which farming can be accessed not just by the wealthy, but by passionate, smart, hardworking people who want to serve, nourish, and sustain, is essential. If we want a diverse group of young people to take over millions of acres of land across this country and farm it safely, healthfully, and profitably, we've got to find an alternative model that rewards farmers not for their heritage, but for their skill and acumen as tenders, managers, and farm businesspeople.

It's not enough to throw money at changing farm practices. We need to change the way we think about farms, farmland, and working in agriculture completely.

When we reframe farming not as a calling or a lifestyle but as a job, we can abandon the vision of farming as destiny, and understand that farms are not philanthropic endeavors, public service providers, or outgrowths of nature, but profit-seeking businesses. This simple change in perspective is transformative. In part because the rest of us know not every business is viable and not every person is well-suited for every job. Building a career is a lifelong journey of understanding personal strengths and weaknesses, likes and dislikes, ideals and boundaries. Few of us regular-job-holding schlubs would think "because Dad did it" a good enough reason to pursue a life's work, much less to shoulder the mantle of an entire identity. And when farms fail or farmers wish to move on, this reframing allows us to understand it for what it is—not the death of an American Dream, but simply a person finding a better fit.

We should strive toward this kind of comfort with turnover in farming because from death comes life. Often, it's only when farms go under and farmland goes up for sale that a chance for real transformation is on the table. Debbie Morrison from Sapsucker described this phenomenon in her community as a rural renaissance.

"Right next to us is a dairy, which used to be what all the farms in this area were," she told me by phone, "But across the way is a grass-fed beef operation, and a lot of places are being converted into vegetable farms and specialty farms. We're really at a turning point for agriculture in this area. The small dairy farms have gone away, and other types of agriculture are coming." This whisper of change, with its implications not just for a different farming system but for rural revitalization, offers hope that there might be an opening for the big team farms version of American agriculture to take hold.

NOW AND THEN

Our vision for American agriculture cannot be a small one. A resilient, survivable tomorrow for America will require farmers who strive to grow healthy, affordable food, create just, livable jobs, and to be good environmental stewards.

If the farmers we have now cannot find their way quickly toward these goals, then it may be in everyone's best interest for them to move on gracefully so other farmers can continue the hard work of change.

The good news is, experts among communities of color are ready to lead the way, and lessons learned beyond agriculture offer powerful tools for creative entrepreneurs looking to run farm businesses differently. Big team farms, as we've seen, are not a new invention, and in many respects don't look too different from startups where workers are compensated with ownership options and the company is owned, at least in part, by the people who run it. The biggest challenge inherent in designing and implementing a better food system then is not in finding or creating new systems that work, but simply in getting necessary resources to the people with the vision.

A big team in a farm setting is relatively rare today, but where they do exist, they are often hard to recognize as farms, but instead appear publicly to be food or fiber businesses. They are often not the poor, hard-scrabble farmers common in media because to run a successful business and provide livable income for owners and employees alike, these operations know they aren't poor, and they don't act like it. These are the farmers Nate Storey described, who started as great small business owners and became great big business owners; growing the numbers of customers they serve and the size of their teams as they went.

Countless benefits are possible to a farming system that consists of diverse teams of people with diverse skills because this transformation *finally* alters the fundamental financial incentives of modern agriculture.

If farms are held, like many other businesses already are, among a group of un-related owners, the incentives to hoard farmland at the cost of the business's profitability fade because partnership in a business is not as heritable as a sole proprietorship. Skilled farmers without assets then have a greater ability to work their way into the business, and a stronger mechanism exists to encourage farmers to retire and rest. Where the farm's financial success is dependent on the skill of its workers rather than their ability to exploit them, particularly those in which workers can become owners, revolutionary incentive exists to abandon bottom-line thinking and operate in a way that creates adequate returns to compensate workers and worker-owners.

That also means big team farms have access to employees with more advanced skill sets, which means more well-trained eyes will be on the lookout for opportunities to make the farm more agile, competitive, and profitable. This would replace the current common denominator in crop marketing on American farms, which revolves around maximizing commodity production despite low demand.

The global pandemic has revealed the deep cracks in our food and agriculture system and how it makes all of us, and especially food system workers, vulnerable. Empowering workers in agriculture, with management if not ownership stakes, creates resiliency, redundancy, buy-in, and more just outcomes. For all these reasons, big team farms can also be expected to be more responsive to consumer needs and to have a greater ability to compensate people appropriately for the time- and skill-intensive work of being environmental stewards.

In short, big team farms are more likely to emphasize the mission and viability of farm businesses over maintenance of personal wealth, are more stable during personnel transitions, make better topline and bottom-line decisions based on economics rather than personal bias, are more able to attract and value the labor they need, and are likely more capable of accessing the economic value of regenerative practices.

The very best news about big team farms is that to help them, all we have to do is get out of their way. Where they have come into existence, they've already conquered the status quo, and in many cases have had to ignore or even actively fight against policy incentives that attempt to contort them into an inherently less viable but more common model. One of the most impactful things that can be done to ensure more big team farms succeed, then, is to withhold our support from their competitors. In a truly level playing field, without the myriad distortions that currently exist in agriculture, it seems likely that big team farms would win on merit. We know because big, diverse teams in other business sectors almost always do.

None of this means every existing family farm is doomed, either. The path to acting more like a big team is open to all, and the more farms that are able to look beyond the independent smallholder model, the more chances we'll have to find the best possible team farm organization for each geography, crop, and market.

Where small farms refuse to leave the fantasy behind, it seems like extreme climate unpredictability in our future will force their hand. Where one operation fails, a new farm will be born. Where that happens, our responsibility as consumers and community, is not to indulge our small family farm fantasies, but instead to offer clear expectations of what it means to be a good farm, and a chance for a diverse community of people, plants, animals, and land to grow.

***

For a deeper discussion of big team farms and the future of growing farms differently, look out for the sequel to Farm (and Other F Words), coming December 2021.

ACKNOWLEDGMENTS

—

This book would not have been possible without the support of a big team of people.

First, this book, and much of my career, would not have been possible if Dr. Sarah Taber had not preceded me. Dr. Taber's work has blazed a trail for a new paradigm in agriculture. I will never be able to thank her enough for her care and patience as a guide and mentor.

The big team also includes many who read early versions and offered thoughtful and provocative feedback: Julia Tanaka, Connie Bowen, Reana Kovalcik, Mackenzie Gross, David Widmar, Silvia Secchi, Nathan Rosenberg, Bryce Stucki, Sarah Nolet, Hopey Fink, Christine Mock, and Rosemary Pritchett-Montavon. Special thanks to my parents, Nancy Galayda-Mock and Ed Mock, who offered tough feedback and support from the earliest stages. I'd also like to thank Jessica Maxwell of the Workers Justice Center of New York, Sara Shipley Hiles of the Missouri School of Journalism, Beth Lyon and Yongyi (Anna) Gu of Cornell University, and Andrew Schots of the Society for Professional Journalists Ethics Committee for offering their invaluable advice in how best to report around the thorny issues related to undocumented workers.

My sincerest thanks as well to the many professionals (and friends) who have influenced my thinking and this journey, often by taking time out of their lives to talk through their own visions for the future of agriculture with me. Those include the many leaders quoted in the book, as well as: Vermont dairy farmer Abbie Corse, food system expert Alison Grantham, farm artist Alissa Welker, Nebraska farmer Clay Govier, *The Checkout* podcast's Errol Schweizer, Duke University professor Gabriel Rosenberg, Nebraska Law's Anthony Schutz, Abigail Sherburne, Christina Crowley-Arklie, Iowa farmer Larry Drenkow, Duke Law professor Lee Miller, *In The Tension*'s Leticia Ochoa Adams, The Union of Concerned Scientists' Ricardo Salvador, Rhishi Pethe, Sarah Nolan, Sally Krueger, Stephen Hohenrieder, Stephanie Pearl, Stephanie Martin, Renate Ware, western artist Lucy Ellis, Selwyn Justice, agtech investor Mark Kahn, Michael Flynn, AgGrad's Tim Hammerich, Montana farmer Todd Eney, Iowa farmer Zack Smith, ag data expert Matthew Meisner, Ohio farmer Vaughn Davis, and Tommy Cress, former Wyoming agriculture teacher who taught me how to have a heart that takes up my whole chest cavity.

Boundless gratitude to the few, strong, incredible journalists on the agriculture and adjacent beats in the US. For all I had ever heard about the competitiveness of professional journalism, these reporters didn't just welcome me into their ranks, they advised, encouraged, and supported me, modeled intrepidness and journalistic ethic, and helped me become the reporter I am today. Thank you to: Catherine Boudreau, Helena Bottemiller Evich, Leah Douglas, Savannah Maher, Boyce Upholt, Caitlin Dewey, Teaganne Finn,

Charlie Mitchell, Clay Masters, Claire Kelloway, Katelyn Rindlisbaker, Madelyn Beck, Jessica Hardin, Leyland Cecco, Steve Davies, Alan Bjerga, Jerry Hagstrom, Chris Clayton, and Bill Tomson.

An extra special thanks to Mallory Carr, the friend who convinced me to leave the Vacaville farm, for always seeing through my rose-colored bullshit. To both Marisha Wick-remsinhe and Amanda Carleton, who taught me about justice when they really, *really* didn't have to, and when I failed to learn, for not giving up on me. Thank you to world-class high school math teacher and improv coach Rick Simineo, who told a sixteen-year-old she could ignore the lesson on Euclid when she published something important enough to be relevant for three thousand years. One year down, two thousand, nine hundred and ninety-nine to go.

Extra thanks to my editor, Joanna Hatzikazakis, whose unfailing encouragement helped this book push past many boundaries. Also thank you to Eric Koester, Bryan Bies, and the entire team at New Degree Press who allowed me tremendous latitude to tell this story the way it needed to be told.

Words are inadequate to fully acknowledge how much Bryan Dombrowski contributed to this work, not only by asking the best questions throughout many edits and providing endless love and encouragement, but also by reminding me to eat during long bouts of writing and by making sure the life we've built together didn't fall apart while I was chasing farm stories.

Finally, I want to acknowledge the many, many people who financially backed the publication of this book and its sequel, and who followed me through the publishing journey and provided invaluable support every step of the way.

These marvelous Big Team Farm people are (alphabetically by first name):

Aaron Alvarado, Abby Dubisar, Abigael McGuire, Abigail Yun, Abram Marr, Adam Brock, Adam Danforth, Adam Gordon, Adam Yarina, Adaugo Ugocha, Addison McTague, Adrianne Brand, Agnes P Cwalina, Aileen Verdun, Alden Lenhart, Alex Carson, Alexander Dale, Alex Dunham, Alex Kazer, Alexander T Huth, Alexander Zajac, Alexandra Jones, Alice Bagley, Alicia Ly, Alicia "Sprout" Symanski, Alison Abbors, Alison Flynn, Alle Grooch, Allen Smart, Alley Swiss, Allison Hadley, Allison Stawara, Allison Tse, Allison Walters, Amalia M. Child, p Amanda Brady Ford, Amanda Cyr, Amanda J. Eller, Amanda Pearson, Amanda Wagstaff, Ameen Lotfi, Amy Crone, Amy Greulich, Amy Halloran, Amy Murray, Amy Yoon, Ana Fochesatto, Anamaria Bell, Anastasia Stier, Andi Hayes, Andras Ferencz, Andrea Vaage, Andreas Shepard, Andrew Akre, Andrew D Palm, Andrew Van Dam, Andrew W Kosick, Andrew Webster, Andrew West, Andreya Piplica, Angela Sheppard, Angela Sun, Anjali Dalal, Iowa farmer Anna Balvance, Anna Lappé, ag scientist Anna Sowa, Anna Tsaur, Anna Wheeler, Anna Zhenova, Anne Holland, Anne Marie Wissman, Anne Thrall Nash, Anusheh Siddiqi, Arabelle Schoenberg, Ari Gold, Ari Lattanzi, Ari Novy, Ariana DeLaurentis, Arnaud Arens, Ashley Alexander, Ashley Colglazier, Ashley Rood, Ashley Woods, Ashley deWilde, Ashly Schilling-Weiner, Aubrey Suter, Audrey Sutton, Colorado farmer Austin Killin, and Avery Pheil.

Ben Goodrich, Bailey Lutz, Bailey Schlegel, Barney Debnam, Barry Mac Devitt, Barton Holcomb, Bauston Wilde, Bayla Gottesman, Beatrice Mora, Bekah Bankson, Ben Capozzi, Ben Evans, Ben Iuliano, Ben Jackle, Ben Jensen, Ben Newman, Ben Penner, Benjamin Alexander, Benjamin

Shankwitz, Benjamin Smith, Beth Haymaker, Beth Satterwhite, Betsy Appleton, Beverly Marshall Saling, Bill Farmilo, Billy Arthur, Blake J Blando, Blake Jacquot, Bob Maertz, Brad Shantz, Bradley Priest, Bradley Santi, Brady Lyles, Brandon Duxbury, Brandon Kirklen, Brandon Ungar, Brant Caley, Brendon Collier, Brett Volz, Brian Bartle, Brian H Roberts, Briana Mills-Walker, Brianna McGuire, Bridget McNassar, Britt Raybould, Brittany Kruger, Brittany O'Brien, Brittney Kupec, Brittany Taylor, and Bryan Schmidt.

Caitie Rountree, Caitlin Germana, Caitlin Maxwell, Caitlin Obom, Caitlin Tucker, Cake Rivara, Camas Davis, Cameron Adamez, Cameron Walkup, Camille Morse Nicholson, Candace Seu, Carl Segerstrom, Carla Ahlschwede, Carly Basinger, Caroline Gorman, Carrie B Sachse, Carrie Holt, Catherine Schnur, Cathryn Henning, Ceci Behgam, Cecile Parrish, Chad Morrow, Chadley Hollas, Chandler Briggs, Charlee Smith, Charles Orr, Charles Purnell, Charlie Watt, Charlotte Morgan, Chelsea Harbach, Chelsea Lawrence, Chris Gillotti, Chris Heinz, Chloe Hartwell, Chris Maiorana, Chris Wallish, Christopher Weisel, Chris Yoder, Christian Gaspar, Christian Tucker, Christina Lood, Christopher Clark, Christopher Hain, Christopher Maxwell, Christopher Porter, Christine Cole, Cindy Warren, Claire Barnes, Claire Kinlaw, Claire Persichetti, Clara Gustafson, Clare Brock, Clare Riesman, Clare Vickers, Clarice Martens, Clemens Gleich, Col Gordon, US Congresswoman Chellie Pingree, Colin Hélie-Harvey, Connor Kilbride Scoltock, Connor Stedman, Cooper Forsman, Costa Boutsikaris, Courtney Guerra, Courtney Young, Craig Murkar, Crystal Gehr, and Crystal Gong.

Daan de Vries, Damon McCormick, Dan Maycock, Dan McCarthy, Dan Meyer, Dana Cabico, Dana

McCormick, Daniel Anthony Coleman, Daniel Golliher, Daniel Merewether, Daniel Miller, Daniel Raleigh, Daniel B. Watts, Danielle Thurow, Danielle Will, Dara Schreiber, David Hall, David Kua, David Lepine, David Thoms, Dayna Burtness, Debra Tropp, DeeAnn Campbell, Deirdre Keller, Derek Silva, Derek Wolf, Derrick Weston, Devin Wright, Diana Egerton-Warburton, Diane Ashworth, Diane Buchwalder, Diane McKenzie, Dinu Ajikutira, Dirk Karis, Doreen Hartzell, Dorian Eder, Douglas Doughty, Douglas Meyer, and Dylan Stein.

E. Begley, EB Witcher, Edmund Hamann, Eileen Flanagan, Elaine Pirie, Elena Bird, Eli Barraza, Elias Berbari, Elizabeth Chen, Elizabeth Cox, Elizabeth Grimm, Elizabeth Thiel, Elizabeth Town, Elizabeth Van Lysal, Elizabeth Wright, Elizabeth Zipf, Ellie Youngblood, Elliot M. Young, Elliott Perkins, Ellyn Ferguson, Emily Bowers, Emily Cho, Emily Lerman, Emily Simpson, Emily Tufts, Emily Shelton, Emma Burgess, Emma Donahoe, Eric Boatti, Eric Booth, Eric Davis, Eric Haseltine, Eric Lagueruela, Eric Lengvenis, Eric Merrill, Eric Schneider, Eric Sherman, Erin Hirte, Erin Morris, Erin Morse, Evan Bell, and EW.

Febin Kachirayil, Fnarf (Steve Thornton), Frances Kelliher, Frank J Graeff III, Frank Spring, and Frannie Miller.

Gaston C. Marian, Gail Langellotto-Rhodaback, Gavin Cornwell, Geoffrey Seelen, George Weld, Ginger Kautz, Glen Hayley, Gordon Edgar, Grace C Gilles, Graham Schaffer, Grant Ennis, Grant Pezeshki, Greg Self, Gregory L. Ludwig, and Géry Debongnie.

Haley Shoaf, Hanna Buechi, Hannah Davis, Hannah Packman, Hannah Phillips, Hannah Tripp, Hannah Dankbar, Hans Weisheimer, Harley Braun, Hawthorn McCracken, Hayden Holbert, Haythem Sanaa, Heather Griffith, Heather

L Johnson, Heidi Samuelson, Helen Cunningham, Helmut Drewes, Holly Giblin, Holly Hammond, and Holly Rippon-Butler.

Ian R. Solberg, Ilsa DeWald, Irene Hamburger, Irina Hynes, Isaac Christensen, and Isabelle Smith.

J. Mark Tebben, Jason Dorsett, JD Cowan, Jennifer Diane Trombley Rohs, Jack Anderson, Jack Reichert, Jacob Mackellar, Jacob Oleshansky, Jacquelin Mosier, Jacqueline Allison, Jacqueline Anderson, Jacquine Stork, James Aimonetti, James Amenta, James Duncan, James Eury, Jenn Bronson, James Fairbairn, James French, James Gaehring, James Jarrett, James Pryor, James Yoo, Jamie Baker, Jamie Goodman, Jamie Russo, Jamie Sipsis, Jamie Wertz, Jane Beauchamp, Jane Jordan, Janelle Cole, Janet R Fleshman, Jaron Curtsinger, Jason Flatt, Jason P Halm, Jean-Francois Caron, Jean-Marc Leclerc, Jeanette Leehr, Jeanne Pineau, Jeff Dearborn, Jeff Hilnbrand, Jeff Jackson, Jeffrey Piestrak, Jeffrey Rothrock, Jeffrey Seale, Jen Liu, Jennie Wolfe, Jennifer Bagley, Jennifer Green, Jennifer Reft, Jeremie Pemberton, Jeremy Weinberger, Jess Yon, Jesse Jacob, Jessica Caroom, Jessica Hulse Dillon, Jessica Woudsma, Jett Utah Watson, Jillian Donatto, Jillian Korolnek, Jim Gruman, Joel Henning, Johanna Oosterwyk, Johanna Whitson, John Costello, John Goldberg, John H Holtz, John Lusk, John Lichten, John Maddux, John Saunders, Johnathan Hettinger, Jon Banner, Jonathan Barnhill, Jonathan Berger, Jonathan E Kauffman, Jonathan Eckman, Jonathan Harris, Jonathan Kitchens, Jonathan P Flothow, Jonathan Pryor, Jordan Scheibel, Jordan Sucher, Jordan Taylor, Joseph Cornelius, Joseph Smith, Josephine Stewart, Josh Goodman, Josh Heling, Josh Mazen, Joshua Gunter, Joshua Rapp, Joshua Stainthorp, Jules Klassen, Julia Kedge, Julia Kuzel, Julia

Loman, Julia Miller, Julia Trzcinski, Julian Peterson, Julie Herlihy, Justin Gentle, and Justin Saret.

KC Crewdson, Kara Siewers, Karen Stillerman, Kari Bernard, Kat Jack, Kat Trent Bertoni, Kate Gragg, Kate Rivara, Kate Stavisky, Katelyn Myhre, Katharine Lee, Kathe Welch, Katherine Boufford, Katherine Davis, Katherine Goss, Katherine Watkins, Kathryn Basinsky, Katie Huszcza, Katie Konstantopoulos, Katie Mazzini, Katieprock, Katy Pepper, Katy Severson, Kellee James, Kelsey Jorissen, Kelsey Rairigh, Kenneth Lowery, Keren Ram, Kevin J. Bavaro, Kevin Chen, Kevin Kosin, Kiel Ortega, Kimberly Harper Coyle, Kimberly Iverson, Kira Sixbery, Kirsten Simmons, Kris Coltvet, Kurt Tsuo, Kyla Bedard, Kyle Hugo, and Kyle Taborski.

Lacey Piekarz, Larry Kearns, Lars Cleary, Laura Baldwin, Laura Jennings, Laura Lee, Laura Nelson, Laurel Halbany, Lauren King, Lauren Salvatore, Lee Carroll, Lee Kuykendall, Levi Kruch, Liane Reeves, Libby Robinette, Linden Huizinga, Lindsay A Steinmann, Lindsay Barnes, Lindsay Harris, Lindsey Higgins, Lindsey Maas, Lisa A Kerr, Lisa McKeag, Lisa Rogers, Livvy Call, Logan Bell, Lora Elliott, Lora L. Abe, Lori Goldberg, Lori Sallet, Lourdes Orlando, Lucas Chan, Lucia Vancura, Lucy Stewart, and Luming Hao.

Mackenzie Muirhead, Mackenzie Worrall, Maddie Lutkewitte, Madeleine Carey, Mae Turner, Maggie McGoldrick, Maia Bailey, Maja Black, Malinda Bernard, Margaret Bauer, Maria Rodale, Marilyn Yarbrough, Mark Fujiwara, Mark Russo, Mark Simon, Markus DeMartini, Martin Verni, Mary Buchanan, Mary Klein, Mary Shelman, Mary Silverstein, Mary von Krusenstiern, Matt Arends, Matt Cordova, Matt Ellison, Matt Parsons, Matt Patterson, Matt Sernett, Matthew Strauss, Matthew Bergene, Matthew David Inglis, Matthew Donald, Matthew Russo, Matthew Wallenstein, Max I Kabat,

Max Lyrata, Max Oliver Thoreson, Maxine Mota, Maxwell Neely-Cohen, Maya Major, Maya Rodale, McCullough Kelly-Willis, Meaghan Burford, Meaghan Sale, Meg Callahan, Meg Mikovits, Megan Brown, Megan Elizabeth Barkdull, Megan Perkins, Megan Tornatore, Megan Tornatore, Megan Tyminski, Meghan Giroux, Meghan Miller Brawley, Melissa Beaty, Melissa Malandrinos, Melissa Seidl, Meredith Bowhers, Meredith Johnson, Meredith Mineo, Michael Braun Hamilton, Michael Dratch, Michael LaHaye, Michael Langford, Michael Richardson, Michael Kliger, Michael Tlusty, Michaela Hoffelmeyer, Michaela Lubbers, Michele Miller, Michele Thorne, Michelle Klieger, Michelle Senar Dressler, Mike Craig, Mina Vafaeezadeh, Miriam Schlessinger, Molly Schintler, Monica J Gandara, Monica Toth, Myron Bruce, and Mzuri Handlin.

Naomi Nelson, Natalie Cantlin, Natalie Fiertz, Natalie McGarry, Natasha Paris, Natasha Wilson, Nate Eitzmann, Nathaniel G. Fenton, Naveen Sikka, Nellie DeHart, Niall Motson, Nicholas Johnson, Nick Beary, Nick Doiron, Nick LaVigne, Nick Lund, Nicolas de la Vega, Nicole Sanders, Nicole Torrico, Niketa Kumar, Nina Bacho, Noah Kippley-Ogman, Noelle Joy, Nolan Monaghan, and Norah Langweiler.

Olivia Taylor-Puckett.

Pam Mack, Pamela H Alexander, Parker Wells, Patrick Pelz, Paul Nguyen, Pete Bergene, Pete Siegel, Peter Coffin, Peter Henry, Peter Schott, Peyton Coles, Phebe Gibson, Philip Dearing, Poppy Davis, and Prescott Paulin.

Rachel Bartunek, Rachel Chalmers, Rachel Detweiler, Rachel Fritz Schaal, Rachel Garner, Rachel King, Rachel Melnick, Rachel Stearns, Raven Fawcett, Ray Starling, Raymond S McKinney, Rebecca Biros, Rebecca Fudge, Rebecca Kaufman, Rebecca Klima, Rebecca Romano, Rebecca Wolf,

Rebekah Brooks, Rebekah Denn, Regnault Thomas, Reid Compton, Renee Vassilos, Ressa Charter, Rian E Wanstreet, Rich Maddux, Rik Smith, River Whitman, Rob Taylor, Rob Wallbridge, Robert Barnett, Robert Erbes, Robert J Bertsch, Robert Jackel, Rory Nussbaumer, Rosa Henritzy, Rosabelle Houdin, Rose Hayden-Smith, Rose Kristoffersen, Rosemary Clark, Russell Knight, Russell Wallack, Ruth Reichl, Ryan Ackett, and Ryan Brink.

Sai Lella, Sally Evans, Sally Lynx, Salman Somjee, Sam Bonney, Sam Dillingham, Samantha Jewel, Samantha Quiñones, and Samuel Kernan. International Council of Sara(h)s representatives: Sara Klausner, Sara Kroopf, Sarah Blanchard, Sarah Campbell, Sarah Corinne, Sarah Goslee, Sarah Hulick, Sarah Knight, and Sarah Sheppard. Saro Schwarzkopf, Scott Metzger, Sean Degrace, Sean Martin, Selena Bryant, Shannon Holder, Shannon Washburn, Shawna Searles, Shayna Sessler, Sheila Morehouse, Sherri Nichols, Siri Erickson-Brown, Sonia Preston, Sophia Rose DeGroot, Spencer Davis, Spencer Moul, Stacie Irwin, Stefanie Hubauer, Stephanie Faires, Stephanie Nielsen, Stephanie Reinert, Stephen Kissinger, Steve Thornton, Steve Thornton, Steve Welker, Steven Johnson, Steven Tomlinson, Susan Kaminski, Susan Langenes, Susan Wilcox, Susan Wilmarth, Suzanne Snyder, and Sven Sielhorst.

TK Zellers, Tad L Wesley, Tamara McLaughlin, Tamara Persaud, Tan Doan, Tanna Sherrill, Tara Waller, Taylor Jones, Taylor Truckey, Terry O'Carroll, Teyler Padberg, Theodora Fan, Thomas Depierre, Thomas Prince, Thomas W Dibble, Thomas Knaust, Tierney Monahan, Tifany Ables, Tiffany Rodriguez, Tim Friesen, Tim Magner, Timmie Escobedo, Timothy Meyers, Tina Lakinger, Toby Vernon, Todd Crocken, Todd G Cavallo, Todd Price, Tom Devol, Tom

Henner, Tom Herman, Tom MacWright, Torin Metz, Tracy Elmore, Trent Fisher, Trishla Jain, Troy Toman, Tyler Eaton, Tyler Isaac.

Udaya Patnaik.

Vanessa Garcia Polanco, Veronica Flores, Vishal Katariya, Vivian Wauters, and Vonnie Estes.

Walker Orr, Wendie Schneider, Wesley A Kuemmel, Whitney Horn, Will Brinkerhoff, Will O'Meara, William Helman, and William Rausch.

Yang Yang.

Zach Menchini, Zach Walchuk, Zak Kamphaus, Zoe Brittain, and Zoe Plakias.

REFERENCES

Abbott, Chuck. 2021. "Agriculture Must be Part of Climate Change Negotiations, says Farm Bureau." *FERN Ag Insider*, January 10, 2021. https://thefern.org/ag_insider/agriculture-must-be-part-of-climate-change-negotiations-says-farm-bureau/.

Adcock, Flynn, David Anderson, and Parr Rosson. 2015. *The Economic Impacts of Immigrant Labor on US Dairy Farms*. College Station, TX: Center for North American Studies, Texas A&M University. https://www.nmpf.org/wp-content/uploads//immigration-survey-090915.pdf.

AFBF (American Farm Bureau Federation). 2020. "AFBF Calls on Lawmakers to Help Farmers Through Food System Shockwave." American Farm Bureau Federation Press Release, June 10, 2020. https://www.fb.org/newsroom/afbf-calls-on-lawmakers-to-help-farmers-through-food-system-shockwave.

Ahearn, Mary Clare. 2011. "Potential Challenges for Beginning Farmers and Ranchers." *Choices*, April 2011. http://choicesmagazine.org/choices-magazine/theme-articles/

innovations-to-support-beginning-farmers-and-ranchers/
potential-challenges-for-beginning-farmers-and-ranchers.

Arax, Mark. 2018. "A Kingdom from Dust." *The California Sunday Magazine,* January 31, 2018. https://story.californiasunday.com/ resnick-a-kingdom-from-dust.

Arcury, Thomas A. and Sara A Quandt. 2009. "The Health and Safety of Farmworkers in the Eastern United States: A Need to Focus on Social Justice." In *Latino Farmworkers in the Eastern United States.* New York: Springer-Verlag. https://doi. org/10.1007/978-0-387-88347-2_1.

Barickman, B.J. 1994. "'A Bit of Land, Which They Call Roça': Slave Provision Grounds in the Bahian Recôncavo, 1780-1860." *The Hispanic American Historical Review* 74 (4) (November) 649-87. https://doi.org/10.1215/00182168-74.4.649.

Bauer, Mary and Meredith Stewart. 2013. "Close to Slavery: Guest-worker Programs in the United States, 2013 Edition." Montgomery, AL: *The Southern Poverty Law Center.* https://www. splcenter.org/sites/default/files/d6_legacy_files/downloads/ publication/SPLC-Close-to-Slavery-2013.pdf.

Biden for President. n.d. "The Biden-Harris Plan to Build Back Better in Rural America." Biden Harris: Battle for the Soul of the Nation. Accessed February 20, 2021. https://joebiden. com/rural-plan/.

Bittman, Mark, Michael Pollan, Ricardo Salvador, and Olivier De Schutter. 2015. "A National Food Policy for the 21st Century." *Food is the New Internet* on Medium, October 6, 2015. https://

medium.com/food-is-the-new-internet/a-national-food-policy-for-the-21st-century-7d323ee7c65f.

Blair, Elizabeth. 2014. "In Confronting Poverty, 'Harvest Of Shame' Reaped Praise And Criticism." *National Public Radio,* May 31, 2014. https://www.npr.org/2014/05/31/317364146/in-confronting-poverty-harvest-of-shame-reaped-praise-and-criticism.

Burchell, Brendan and Ala Hughes. 2006. *The Stigma of Failure: An International Comparison of Failure Tolerance and Second Chancing.* Working Paper No. 334 (December). Cambridge, United Kingdom: Centre for Business Research, University of Cambridge. https://www.researchgate.net/publication/4801098_The_stigma_of_failure_An_international_comparison_of_failure_tolerance_and_second_chancing.

Calo, Adam. 2020. "The Yeoman Myth: A Troubling Foundation of the Beginning Farmer Movement." *Gastronomica,* 20, no. 2. Summer 2020. 12-29.

Carney, Judith A. 1993. "From Hands to Tutors: African Expertise in the South Carolina Rice Economy." *Agricultural History* 67 (3) (Summer): 1-30. https://www.jstor.org/stable/3744227?refreqid=excelsior%3A5f9c1fe5d68dd7060a0067b92dd47161&seq=1.

Charles, Dan. 2020. "Farmers Got A Government Bailout In 2020, Even Those Who Didn't Need It." *National Public Radio,* December 30, 2020. https://www.npr.org/2020/12/30/949329557/farmers-got-a-government-bailout-in-2020-even-those-who-didnt-need-it.

Clark, Andy, ed. 2012. *Managing Cover Crops Profitably, 3rd Edition*. Sustainable Ag Research and Education (SARE) program handbook series. June 2012. https://www.sare.org/publications/managing-cover-crops-profitably/benefits-of-cover-crops/.

Cochrane, Willard W. 1981. *The Development of American Agriculture: A Historical Analysis*. Minneapolis, MN: University of Minnesota Press.

Confederated Tribes and Bands of the Yakama Nation. n.d. "Tribal Enterprises." Accessed January 29, 2021. https://www.yakama.com/tribal-enterprises/.

Connor, Tom. 2019. "Trade Wars, Climate Change Plunge the Family Farm into Crisis. Is It an Endangered American Institution?" *CNBC Evolve*, November 2, 2019. https://www.cnbc.com/2019/11/02/trade-wars-climate-change-plunge-the-family-farm-into-crisis.html.

Costa, Daniel and Philip Martin. 2020. "How Much Would it Cost Consumers to Give Farmworkers a Significant Raise?" *Working Economics Blog*, October 15, 2020. https://www.epi.org/blog/how-much-would-it-cost-consumers-to-give-farmworkers-a-significant-raise-a-40-increase-in-pay-would-cost-just-25-per-household/.

Costa, Daniel, Philip Martin, and Zachariah Rutledge. 2020. *Federal Labor Standards Enforcement in Agriculture*. Washington, DC: Economic Policy Institute. https://www.epi.org/publication/federal-labor-standards-enforcement-in-agriculture-data-reveal-the-biggest-violators-and-raise-new-questions-about-how-to-improve-and-target-efforts-to-protect-farmworkers/.

Craig, Tim. 2017. "Deaths of Farmworkers in Cow Manure Ponds Put Oversight of Dairy Farms into Question." *Washington Post,* September 24, 2017. https://www.washingtonpost.com/national/deaths-of-farmworkers-in-cow-manure-ponds-put-oversight-of-dairy-farms-into-question/2017/09/24/da4f1bae-8813-11e7-961d-2f373b3977ee_story.html.

CRS (Congressional Research Service). 2019. "Farm Policy: Comparison of 2018 and 2019 MFP Programs," August 12, 2019, 1. https://crsreports.congress.gov/product/pdf/IF/IF11289.

Daniel, Pete. 2013. *Dispossession: Discrimination against African American Farmers in the Age of Civil Rights.* Chapel Hill, NC: The University of North Carolina Press.

Devine, Robert S. 1995. "The Trouble with Dams." *The Atlantic Monthly,* https://www.theatlantic.com/past/docs/politics/environ/dams.htm.

Dewey, Caitlin. 2017. "The Surprising Number of American Adults Who Think Chocolate Milk Comes from Brown Cows." *The Washington Post,* June 15, 2017. https://www.washingtonpost.com/news/wonk/wp/2017/06/15/seven-percent-of-americans-think-chocolate-milk-comes-from-brown-cows-and-thats-not-even-the-scary-part/.

Dickerman, Charles W. 1868. *How to Make the Farm Pay; or The Farmer's Book of Practical Information on Agriculture, Stock Raising, Fruit Culture, Special Crops, Domestic Economy & Family Medicine.* Philadelphia, PA: Zeigler, McCurdy & Co.

Dimitri, Carolyn, Anne Effland, and Neilson Conklin. 2005. *The 20th Century Transformation of US Agriculture and Farm Policy*. Information Bulletin Number 3 (June). Washington: DC, United States Department of Agriculture, Economic Research Service. https://www.ers.usda.gov/webdocs/publications/44197/13566_eib3_1_.pdf?v=679.8.

DOL WHD (United States Department of Labor Wage and Hour Division). 2020. *Fact Sheet #12: Agricultural Employers Under the Fair Labor Standards Act (FLSA)*. Revised January 2020. Washington, DC: United States Department of Labor Wage and Hour Division. https://www.dol.gov/sites/dolgov/files/WHD/legacy/files/whdfs12.pdf.

DOT IRS (Department of the Treasury Internal Revenue Service). 2020. "Farmer's Tax Guide." Publication 223, Cat No. 11049L. October 15, 2020. https://www.irs.gov/pub/irs-pdf/p225.pdf.

Edwards, Chris. 2018. "Agricultural Subsidies." Downsizing the Federal Government. April 16, 2018. https://www.downsizinggovernment.org/agriculture/subsidies#_edn26.

Elworthy, Forbes. 2020. "Volatility to Explain High Historic Farmland Returns." *The Property Chronicle,* August 5, 2020. https://www.propertychronicle.com/volatility-explain-high-historical-farmland-returns/#mailing-signup.

EWG (Environmental Working Group) Farm Subsidy Database (Glen Govier & Sons; accessed February 21, 2021a). https://farm.ewg.org/persondetail.php?custnumber=A06365802.

EWG (Environmental Working Group) Farm Subsidy Database (John N Mills & Sons; accessed February 21, 2021b). https://farm.ewg.org/persondetail.php?custnumber=A08735957.

Faleide, Nathan. 2017. "Mirror Mirror on the Wall, Who is the Most Trusted Ag Advisor of Them All?" *PrecisionAg*, April 4, 2017. https://www.precisionag.com/market-watch/mirror-mirror-on-the-wall-who-is-the-most-trusted-ag-advisor-of-them-all/.

Farm Aid. n.d. "Our Work." Accessed February 4, 2021. https://www.farmaid.org/our-work/.

Farm Bureau. n.d. "2018 Farm Bill: Issue at a Glance." Accessed January 15, 2021. https://www.fb.org/issues/farm-policy/the-2018-farm-bill/.

Farmworker Justice. n.d. "What We Do: US Labor Law for Farmers." Accessed January 10, 2021. https://www.farmworkerjustice.org/advocacy_program/us-labor-law-for-farmworkers/.

Fields, Scott. 2004. "The Fat of the Land: Do Agricultural Subsidies Foster Poor Health?" *Environews* 112 (14) (October 2004): 820–823. https://doi.org/10.1289/ehp.112-a820.

Food Print. n.d. "FoodPrint Issue: How Industrial Agriculture Affects Our Soil." Food Print. Accessed February 28, 2021. https://foodprint.org/issues/how-industrial-agriculture-affects-our-soil/.

Friends of Bernie Sanders. n.d. "Issues: Revitalizing Rural America." Bernie Sanders for President. Accessed February 20, 2021. https://berniesanders.com/issues/revitalizing-rural-america/.

GBH Forum Network. 2010. "Nobel Prize Lecture by Professor Elinor Ostrom Recipient of the 2009 Sveriges Riksbank Prize in Economic Sciences." YouTube video, February 16, 2010, 1:02:03. https://www.youtube.com/watch?v=T6OgRki5SgM.

Gila River Farms. n.d. "Mission." Accessed January 29, 2021. https://gilariverfarmssales.com/.

Gordon-Reed, Annette and Peter S. Onuf. 2016. *"Most Blessed of the Patriarchs": Thomas Jefferson and the Empire of the Imagination.* New York: W. W. Norton & Company, Inc.

Greer, Allan. 2012. "Commons and Enclosure in the Colonization of North America," *The American Historical Review* 117 (2) (April): 365–386. https://doi.org/10.1086/ahr.117.2.365.

Gundersen, Craig and Susan Offutt. 2005. "Farm Poverty and Safety Nets." *American Journal of Agricultural Economics* 87, no. 4. (November 2005): 885–899. https://naldc.nal.usda.gov/download/6832/PDF.

Haden, Jeff. 2020. "64 Years Ago, Ray Kroc Made a Decision That Completely Transformed McDonald's. The Rest Is History." *Inc.*, November 16, 2020. https://www.inc.com/jeff-haden/64-years-ago-ray-kroc-made-a-decision-that-completely-transformed-mcdonalds-rest-is-history.html.

Hardin, Garrett. 1968. "The Tragedy of the Commons." *Science* 162 (3859) (December): 1243-1248. https://doi.org/10.1126/science.162.3859.1243.

Haskell's The Wine People!. n.d. "Import: Yellow Belly Hard Apple Cider 22oz." Accessed February 21, 2021. https://www.haskells.com/yellow-belly-hard-apple-cider-22oz.

Hayes, Jared. 2020. "Members of Congress Got Nearly $16 Million in Farm Subsidies and Trade War Bailout," *Environmental Working Group AgMag*, October 20, 2020. https://www.ewg.org/agmag/2020/10/members-congress-got-nearly-16-million-farm-subsidies-and-trade-war-bailout.

Holt-Giménez, Eric Annie Shattuck, Miguel Altieri, Hans Herren and Steve Gliessman. 2012. "We Already Grow Enough Food for 10 Billion People ... and Still Can't End Hunger." *Journal of Sustainable Agriculture* 36, no. 6. 595-598. http://dx.doi.org/10.1080/10440046.2012.695331.

Horst, Megan and Amy Marion. 2018. "Racial, Ethnic and Gender Inequities in Farmland Ownership and Farming in the US" *Agriculture and Human Values* 36 (October): 1–16. https://doi.org/10.1007/s10460-018-9883-3.

Hurt, R. Douglas. 1987. *Indian Agriculture in America: Prehistory to the Present*. Lawrence, KS: University Press of Kansas.

Investing in Regenerative Agriculture and Food. 2020. "Chris Newman on Busting the Single Family Farm Myth and Why Indigenous Collectives are the Way to Go." Podcast. September 29, 2020, 56:37. https://investinginregenerativeagriculture. com/2020/09/29/chris-newman/.

Johansen, Bruce E. 1982. *Forgotten Founders: How the American Indian Helped Shape Democracy*. Boston, MA: The Harvard Common Press.

John F. Kennedy Presidential Library and Museum. n.d. "Remarks of Senator John F. Kennedy at the Jefferson-Jackson Day Dinner, Bismarck, North Dakota, April 11, 1958." John F. Kennedy Presidential Library and Museum. Accessed February 21, 2021. https://www.jfklibrary.org/archives/other-resources/john-f-kennedy-speeches/bismarck-nd-19580411.

Johnson, Benjamin. 2020. *Land Value and Soil Quality: An Untapped Incentive Structure*. Climate Policy Brief No. 13 (June). Medford, MA: Global Development and Environment Institute, Tufts University. https://sites.tufts.edu/gdae/files/2020/06/Ben-Policy-Brief-13.pdf?customize_changeset_uuid=01572015-53dc-482f-9996-f6f6aaec6726&customize_autosaved=on&customize_messenger_channel=preview-1.

Katchova, Ani and Mary Clare Ahearn. 2017. "Farm Entry and Exit from US Agriculture." *Agricultural Finance Review* 77 (1) (May): 50-63. https://doi.org/10.1108/AFR-03-2016-0021.

Karst, Tom. 2018. "Farm Size Steadily Rising for Fruit and Vegetable Growers." *The Packer*, March 21, 2018. https://www.thepacker.com/news/industry/farm-size-steadily-rising-fruit-and-vegetable-growers.

Key, Nigel and Greg Lyons. 2019. *An Overview of Beginning Farmers and Ranchers.* Economic Brief Number 29 (September). Washington, DC. United States Department of Agriculture, Economic Research Service. 2019. https://www.usda.gov/sites/default/files/documents/ERS%20Report-Nigel%20Key.pdf.

Key, Nigel and Michael J. Roberts. 2007. *Commodity Payments, Farm Business Survival, and Farm Size Growth.* Report Number 51 (November 2007). Washington, DC: United States Department of Agriculture Economic Research. https://www.ers.usda.gov/webdocs/publications/45923/12240_err51_1_.pdf?v=9505#:~:text=The%20analysis%20indicates%20that%2C%20at,of%20farm%20survival%20and%20growth.

Khafipour, E., S. Li, H.M. Tun, H. Derakhshani, S. Moossavi, J.C. Plaizier. 2016. "Effects of Grain Feeding on Microbiota in the Digestive Tract of Cattle." *Animal Frontiers* 6 (2) (April): 13–19. https://doi.org/10.2527/af.2016-0018.

Kling, Catherine L. Yiannis Panagopoulos, Sergey S. Rabotyagov, Adriana Valcu-Lisman, Philip W. Gassman, Todd D. Campbell, Michael J. White, et al. 2014. "LUMINATE: Linking Agricultural Land Use, Local Water Quality and Gulf of Mexico Hypoxia." *European Review of Agricultural Economics* 41 (3) (June): 431–459. https://doi.org/10.1093/erae/jbu009.

Koerth, Maggie. 2016. "Big Farms Are Getting Bigger and Most Small Farms Aren't Really Farms At All." *FiveThirtyEight,* November 17, 2016. https://fivethirtyeight.com/features/big-farms-are-getting-bigger-and-most-small-farms-arent-really-farms-at-all/.

LaCanne, Claire E. and Jonathan G. Lundgren. 2018. "Regenerative Agriculture: Merging Farming and Natural Resource Conservation Profitably." *PeerJ* 6 (4428) (February). https://doi.org/10.7717/peerj.4428.

Last Week Tonight. 2015. "Chickens: Last Week Tonight with John Oliver (HBO)." Video, May 18, 2015, 18:21. https://www.youtube.com/watch?v=X9wHzt6gBgI.

Lattman, Peter. 2006. "The Origins of Justice Stewart's 'I Know It When I See It.'" *Wall Street Journal*, September 27, 2006. https://www.wsj.com/articles/BL-LB-4558.

Lehner, Peter H. and Nathan A. Rosenberg. 2019. "Chapter 30: Agriculture." In *Legal Pathways to Deep Decarbonization in the United States,* edited by Michael B. Gerrard & John Dernbach, 772-822. Washington, DC: Environmental Law Institute. https://ssrn.com/abstract=3361393.

Leonard, Kimberlee. 2019. "How to Use a Small Farm for Tax Write Offs." *Small Business Chronicle,* February 12, 2019. https://smallbusiness.chron.com/use-small-farm-tax-write-offs-15880.html.

LII (Legal Information Institute). n.d. "29 CFR § 780.307 Exemption for Employer's Immediate Family." Legal Information Institute, Cornell Law School. Accessed January 21, 2021. https://www.law.cornell.edu/cfr/text/29/780.307#:~:text=Section%2013(a).

Lueger, Tim. 2019. "The Principle of Population and the Malthusian Trap." *Darmstadt Discussion Papers in Economics* 232 (2018): 1-31. http://dx.doi.org/10.2139/ssrn.3492297.

Luna, Guadalupe T. 1999. "An Infinite Distance?: Agricultural Exceptionalism and Agricultural Labor." *University of Pennsylvania Journal of Labor and Employment Law* 1 (2) (Winter): 487-510. https://scholarship.law.upenn.edu/jbl/vol1/iss2/5.

Lundahl, Audrey. 2021. "US Permaculture and the Legacy of Colonizing Ideas." In *Conversations with Food*, edited by Dorothy Chansky and Sarah W. Tracy, 111-124. Wilmington, DE: Vernon Press.

Mann, Charles C. 2005. *1491: New Revelations of the Americas before Columbus*. New York: Knopf.

Marginal Revolution University. 2019. "Elinor Ostrom | Women in Economics," YouTube video, Feb 12, 2019, 1:41. https://www.youtube.com/watch?v=BDEAgmklNyE&feature=youtu.be.

Matsumoto, Valerie J. 1993. *Farming the Home Place: A Japanese American Community in California*. Ithaca, NY: Cornell University Press.

McCarthy, Bonnie. 2019. "Life on the 'Biggest Little Farm': Behind the Scenes of a Biodynamic Blockbuster." *Los Angeles Times,* May 10, 2019. https://www.latimes.com/home/la-hm-biggest-little-farm-documentary-apricot-lane-biodynamic-farm-20190510-story.html.

McElroy, Wendy. 2012. "The Enclosure Acts and the Industrial Revolution." *The Future of Freedom Foundation,* March 8, 2012. https://www.fff.org/explore-freedom/article/enclosure-acts-industrial-revolution/.

Meyer, Mary and Julie Weisenhorn. 2019. "Planting and Maintaining a Prairie Garden." *University of Minnesota Extension.* Reviewed in 2019. https://extension.umn.edu/planting-and-growing-guides/planting-and-maintaining-prairie-garden.

Miller, Dan. 2020. "The Pulse of Rural America." *DTN Progressive Farmer,* December 2020, 14.

Morgan, Edmund S. 1972. "Slavery and Freedom: The American Paradox." *The Journal of American History* 59 (1): 5-29. https://doi.org/10.2307/1888384.

Murdock, Deroy. 2018. "It's Time to Stop Bailing Out Rich, Famous, and Dead Farmers." *National Review,* June 14, 2018. https://www.nationalreview.com/2018/06/agricultural-subsidies-too-many-recipients-are-rich-famous-dead/.

Moskowitz, Peter. 2014. "Small Farms, Big Problems: Labor Crisis Goes Ignored in Idyllic Setting." *Al Jazeera America,* July 29, 2014. http://america.aljazeera.com/articles/2014/7/29/small-farms-labor.html.

The National Archives (UK). n.d. "Currency Convertor, 1270 to 2017." Accessed January 15, 2021. https://www.nationalarchives.gov.uk/currency-converter/#currency-result.

National Archive: Founders Online. n.d. "From Benjamin Franklin to Peter Collinson, 9 May 1753." Accessed February 21, 2021. https://founders.archives.gov/documents/Franklin/01-04-02-0173.

National Archives: Founders Online. n.d. "From Thomas Jefferson to George Washington, 14 August 1787." Accessed February 21, 2021. https://founders.archives.gov/documents/Jefferson/01-12-02-0040.

Navajo Agricultural Products. n.d. "History." Accessed January 29, 2021. https://napi.navajopride.com/history/.

NCGA (National Corn Growers Association). n.d. "Corn Usage By Segment 2019." World of Corn. Accessed January 15, 2021. http://www.worldofcorn.com/#corn-usage-by-segment.

Neeley, Todd. 2019. "More Farms Turn to Bankruptcy in 2019." *DTN Progressive Farmer*, February 3, 2020. https://www.dtnpf.com/agriculture/web/ag/news/farm-life/article/2020/02/03/chapter-12-bankruptcy-filings-grow#:~:text=There%20were%20595%20Chapter%2012,just%20below%202.99%20in%202011.

Neff, Zama. 2011. "Child Farmworkers in the United States: A 'Worst Form of Child Labor.'" *Human Rights Watch*, November 17, 2011. https://www.hrw.org/news/2011/11/17/child-farmworkers-united-states-worst-form-child-labor.

Nickerson, Cynthia, Mitchell Morehart, Todd Kuethe, Jayson Beckman, Jennifer Ifft, and Ryan Williams. 2012. *Trends in US Farmland Values and Ownership*. Economic Information Bulletin No. 92. Washington, DC: US Department of Agriculture, Economic Research Service. https://www.ers.usda.gov/webdocs/publications/44656/16748_eib92_2_.pdf?v=8636.6.

NSAC (National Sustainable Ag Coalition). 2016. "Land Tenure and Turnover: How Are Beginning Farmers Affected?" *National Sustainable Ag Coalition Blog*, September 8, 2016. https://sustainableagriculture.net/blog/land-tenure-beginning-farmers/.

NSAC (National Sustainable Ag Coalition). 2019. "2017 Census of Agriculture Drilldown: Conservation and Energy." *National Sustainable Ag Coalition's Blog*, June 19, 2019. https://sustainableagriculture.net/blog/2017-census-of-agriculture-drilldown-conservation-and-energy/#tillage.

NYS DOH (New York State Department of Health). 2016. "Part 15, Migrant Farmworker Housing." Last Updated May 2016. https://www.health.ny.gov/regulations/nycrr/title_10/part_15/#s151.

Ogletree, Kelsey. 2018. "Hutterites: The Small Religious Colonies Entwined with Montana's Haute Cuisine." *National Public Radio*, July 17, 2018. https://www.npr.org/sections/the-salt/2018/07/17/626543100/hutterites-the-small-religious-colonies-entwined-with-montanas-haute-cuisine.

Okie, William Thomas. 2016. *The Georgia Peach: Culture, Agriculture, and Environment in the American South.* Cambridge, UK: Cambridge University Press.

Payne, Emily. 2019. "Regenerative Agriculture Is Getting More Mainstream. But How Scalable Is It?" *AgFunder News*, May 28, 2019. https://agfundernews.com/regenerative-agriculture-is-getting-more-mainstream-but-how-scalable-is-it.html.

PBS. 2012. "Slavery by Another Name." Video, 2:03. February 12, 2012. https://www.pbs.org/tpt/slavery-by-another-name/themes/sharecropping/.

PBS News Hour. 2019. "How Southern Black Farmers Were Forced from Their Land, and Their Heritage." *PBS News Hour,* August 13, 2019. https://www.pbs.org/newshour/show/how-southern-black-farmers-were-forced-from-their-land-and-their-heritage.

Peacing it All Together. 2019. "Resurrect Eloheh." Podcast, 32:55. https://www.peacingitalltogether.com/podcast/2019/4/29/episode-40-ressurect-eloheh.

Perea, Juan F. 2011. "The Echoes of Slavery: Recognizing the Racist Origins of the Agricultural and Domestic Worker Exclusion from the National Labor Relations Act." *Ohio State Law Journal* 72, no. 1. 95-138. 2011. https://lawecommons.luc.edu/cgi/viewcontent.cgi?article=1150&context=facpubs.

Pirog, Rich S. and John C. Tyndall. 1999. "Comparing Apples to Apples: An Iowa Perspective on Apples and Local Food Systems." *Leopold Center Pubs and Papers* 1. http://lib.dr.iastate.edu/leopold_pubspapers/1.

Plumer, Brad. 2015. "Map: Here's how much each country spends on food." *Vox.* August 19, 2015. https://www.vox.com/2014/7/6/5874499/map-heres-how-much-every-country-spends-on-food.

Pollan, Michael. 2006. *The Omnivore's Dilemma: A Natural History of Four Meals.* New York: Penguin Group.

Polyface Farms. n.d. "Apprenticeships and Summer Stewardship." Accessed January 21, 2021. https://www.polyfacefarms.com/apprenticeship/.

Post, Paul. 2019. "Farmers: New York Labor Law a Bad Deal." *Lancaster Farming,* July 26, 2019. https://www.lancasterfarming.com/news/northern_edition/farmers-new-york-labor-law-a-bad-deal/article_60f17878-f131-5bf9-b242-070839a57222.html.

Poteete, Amy R., Marco A. Janssen, Elinor Ostrom. 2010. *Working Together: Collective Action, the Commons, and Multiple Methods in Practice.* Princeton, NJ: Princeton University Press.

Purdy, Chase. 2018. "The Planet Produces More Than Enough Food, Just Not the Kind People Need." *Quartz,* October 30, 2018. https://qz.com/1442190/the-planet-produces-more-than-enough-food-just-not-the-kind-people-need/.

Rabin, Jack. 2010. "Excess Farm Indebtedness: Not a Sustainable Practice." *Sustainable Farming on the Fringe,* Rutgers University. October 15, 2010. https://sustainable-farming.rutgers.edu/excess-farm-debt-not-sustainable/.

Ralph, Pat. 2018. "A Goat Herd Is Helping Trump Pay Tens of Thousands of Dollars Less in Property Taxes on His New Jersey Properties." *Business Insider,* August 11, 2018. https://www.businessinsider.com/goats-helping-trump-pay-less-taxes-new-jersey-2018-8.

Reveal. 2017. "Losing Ground." Podcast, 50:47. July 1, 2017. https://revealnews.org/episodes/losing-ground/.

Rice, Stian. 2019. "Farmers Turn to Prisons to Fill Labor Needs." *High Country News,* June 12, 2019. https://www.hcn.org/articles/agriculture-farmers-turn-to-prisons-labor-to-fill-labor-needs.

Roos, Debbie. 2020. "Community Supported Agriculture (CSA) Resource Guide for Farmers." Growing Small Farms. Last updated December 2020. https://growingsmallfarms.ces.ncsu.edu/growingsmallfarms-csaguide/.

Rosenberg, Nathan. 2017. "Farmers Who Don't Farm: The Curious Rise of the Zero-Sales Farmer," *Journal of Agriculture, Food Systems, and Community Development.* Advance online publication. https://ssrn.com/abstract=3104703.

Rosenberg, Nathan and Bryce Stucki, 2021a. "Chapter 2: Beyond the Perpetual Farm Crisis." Currently unpublished chapter, March 1, 2021.

Rosenberg, Nathan and Bryce Stucki, 2021b. "LPE Post 1 24." Current unpublished blog, March 1, 2021.

Ram Trucks. 2013. "Farmer | Ram Trucks." Video, February 3, 2013. 2:02. https://www.youtube.com/watch?v=AMpZoTGjbWE.

Riley, M. P. and Stewart, J. R. 1966. *The Hutterites: South Dakota's Communal Farmers.* Paper 531. Brookings, SD: South Dakota State University. http://openprairie.sdstate.edu/agexperiment-sta_bulletins/531.

Rodman, Sarah O., Colleen L. Barry, Megan L. Clayton, Shannon Frattaroli, Roni A. Neff, and Lainie Rutkow. 2016. "Agricultural

Exceptionalism at the State Level: Characterization of Wage and Hour Laws for US Farmworkers." *Journal of Agriculture, Food Systems, and Community Development* 6 (2): 89–110. http://dx.doi.org/10.5304/jafscd.2016.062.013.

Rosenberg, Nathan. 2017. "Farmers Who Don't Farm: The Curious Rise of the Zero-Sales Farmer," *Journal of Agriculture, Food Systems, and Community Development*. Advance online publication. http://dx.doi.org/10.5304/jafscd.2017.074.005.

Ruhl, J.B. 2000. "Farms, Their Environmental Harms, and Environmental Laws." *Ecology Law Quarterly* 27 (263): 263-350. https://scholarship.law.vanderbilt.edu/faculty-publications/472.

Rural Migration News. 2020. "Labor in Fruit and Vegetable Agriculture." *Rural Migration News* (blog), November 20, 2020. https://migration.ucdavis.edu/rmn/blog/post/?id=2497.

Sanderson, Matthew R, Burke Griggs, and Jacob A. Miller. 2020. "Farmers are Depleting the Ogallala Aquifer Because the Government Pays Them to Do It." *The Counter*, November 19, 2020. https://thecounter.org/ogallala-aquifer-farmers-great-plains-drought-water-access-usda/.

Sapsucker Farms. n.d. "2021 CSA." Accessed January 15, 2021. https://sapsuckerfarms.com/2021-csa.

SARE (Sustainable Ag Research and Education). n.d. "Cover Crop Economics: When Incentive Payments are Received for Cover Crop Use." Accessed January 15, 2021. https://www.sare.org/publications/cover-crop-economics/an-in-depth-look-at-management-situations-where-cover-crops-pay-off-faster/

when-incentive-payments-are-received-for-cover-crop-
use/#:~:text=The%20majority%20of%20states%20have,rate%20
below%20%2450%20per%20acre.

Schuman, Michael. 2017. "History of Child Labor in the United
States—Part 1: Little Children Working," *Monthly Labor
Review*. US Bureau of Labor Statistics. January 2017. https://
doi.org/10.21916/mlr.2017.1.

Shapiro, Ariel. 2021. "America's Biggest Owner of Farmland Is
Now Bill Gates." *Forbes*, January 14, 2021. https://www.forbes.
com/sites/arielshapiro/2021/01/14/americas-biggest-owner-of-
farmland-is-now-bill-gates-bezos-turner/?sh=726b986b6096.

Sharespost, n.d. "Plenty IPO." Accessed February 28, 2021. https://
sharespost.com/plenty_ipo/#:~:text=It%20has%20been%20
widely%20reported,valuation%20of%20over%20%241%20bil-
lion.

Smith, Ron. 2014. "Farm-Related Childhood Deaths Are down,
but Still Too Many." *Farm Progress*, June 2, 2014. https://www.
farmprogress.com/equipment/farm-related-childhood-deaths-
are-down-still-too-many.

Smith, Vincent H., Joseph W. Glauber, Barry K. Goodwin, and
Daniel A. Sumner. 2017. *Agricultural Policy in Disarray: Reform-
ing the Farm Bill—An Overview*. Washington, DC: American Enterprise Institute. https://www.aei.org/wp-content/
uploads/2017/10/Agricultural-Policy-in-Disarray.pdf?x88519.

Semuels, Alana. 2016. "The Graying of Rural America." *The Atlantic*, June 2, 2016. https://www.theatlantic.com/business/archive/2016/06/the-graying-of-rural-america/485159/.

Semuels, Alana. 2019. "'They're Trying to Wipe Us off the Map.' Small American Farmers Are Nearing Extinction." *Time*, November 27, 2019. https://time.com/5736789/small-american-farmers-debt-crisis-extinction/#:~:text=But%20it%20has%20been%20declining,and%20a%20red%20barn%20but.

Stephenson, Kurt, Sarah Chase-Walsh, Alyssa Lindrose, Julie Worley, John Ignosh. 2016. *Virginia Citizen's Guide to Environmental Credit Trading Programs: An Overview.* Publication ANR-173P. Blacksburg, VA: Virginia Cooperative Extension. https://www.pubs.ext.vt.edu/content/dam/pubs_ext_vt_edu/ANR/ANR-173/ANR-173-PDF.pdf.

Sullivan, J. R. 2018. "America's Farmers Are in Crisis, and They're Looking to Trump for Relief." *The New Yorker,* January 23, 2018. https://www.newyorker.com/news/news-desk/americas-farmers-are-in-crisis-and-theyre-looking-to-trump-for-relief.

Sullivan, Julie. 2020. "Comparing Characteristics and Selected Expenditures of Dual- and Single-Income Households with Children." *Monthly Labor Review.* US Bureau of Labor Statistics. September 2020. https://doi.org/10.21916/mlr.2020.19.

Tarver, Eva. 2020. "Income Tax vs. Capital Gains Tax: What's the Difference?" *Investopedia*, Last updated December 31, 2020. https://www.investopedia.com/ask/answers/052015/what-difference-between-income-tax-and-capital-gains-tax.asp.

Team Warren. 2019. "The New Farm Economy." *Team Warren* on Medium, August 7, 2019. https://medium.com/@teamwarren/a-new-farm-economy-8db50faco551.

Thomas Jefferson Monticello. n.d. "Jefferson Quotes and Family Letters: Extract from Thomas Jefferson to Thomas Pinckney." Accessed February 21, 2021. https://tjrs.monticello.org/letter/159#X3184736.

Trump White House n.d. "Archives Search Results: Farm." Accessed February 27, 2021. https://trumpwhitehouse.archives.gov/search/?s=farm.

UFW (United Farm Workers). n.d. "UFW History." Accessed January 21, 2021. https://ufw.org/research/history/ufw-history/.

United States Senate. n.d. S.v. "Entitlement." Accessed January 15, 2021. https://www.senate.gov/reference/glossary_term/entitlement.htm.

The Urban Institute. 2017. "Features: Nine Charts about Wealth Inequality in America (Updated)." Last Updated October 5, 2017. https://apps.urban.org/features/wealth-inequality-charts/.

US CIS (United States Citizenship and Immigration Services). 2021. "H-2A Temporary Agricultural Workers." Last updated on January 12, 2021.https://www.uscis.gov/working-in-the-united-states/temporary-workers/h-2a-temporary-agricultural-workers.

US Congressman Antonio Delgado. 2019. "Delgado's Bipartisan Family Farmer Relief Act Signed Into Law." US Congressman

Antonio Delgado Press Release. August 26, 2019. US Congressman Antonio Delgado website. https://delgado.house.gov/media/press-releases/delgado-s-bipartisan-family-farmer-relief-act-signed-law.

USDA (United States Department of Agriculture). 1935. *Farms and Livestock - Number of Farms, Farm Acreage, Value of Farm Land and Buildings, and Livestock on Farms and Ranches in the United States: 1840 to 1935.* 1935 Census Publications. Washington, DC: United States Department of Agriculture. http://lib-usda-05.serverfarm.cornell.edu/usda/AgCensusImages/1935/01/49/1515/Table-01.pdf.

USDA ERS (United States Department of Agriculture Economic Research Service). n.d. "Farm Household Income and Characteristics, Mean and Median Farm Operator Household Income and Ratio of Farm Household to USHousehold Income, 1960-2019." Accessed January 8, 2021. https://www.ers.usda.gov/webdocs/DataFiles/48870/table13.xlsx?v=5526.6.

USDA ERS (United States Department of Agriculture Economic Research Service). n.d. "Requirements for Agricultural Employers Under the Major Federal Employment Tax Laws." Accessed February 21, 2021. https://www.ers.usda.gov/webdocs/publications/41928/19066_ah719k_1_.pdf?v=0.

USDA ERS (United States Department of Agriculture Economic Research Service). 2019a. "Conservation Programs." Last updated September 23, 2019. https://www.ers.usda.gov/topics/natural-resources-environment/conservation-programs/.

USDA ERS (United States Department of Agriculture Economic Research Service). 2019b. "Health Insurance Coverage." Last updated November 27, 2019. https://www.ers.usda.gov/topics/farm-economy/farm-household-well-being/health-insurance-coverage/.

USDA ERS (United States Department of Agriculture Economic Research Service). 2020a. "Farm Labor." Last Updated April 22, 2020. https://www.ers.usda.gov/topics/farm-economy/farm-labor/.

USDA ERS (United States Department of Agriculture Economic Research Service). 2020b. "Farmland Value." Last updated November 2, 2020. https://www.ers.usda.gov/topics/farm-economy/land-use-land-value-tenure/farmland-value/.

USDA ERS (United Stated Department of Agriculture Economic Research Service). 2020c. "Income and Wealth in Context: Farm Household Wealth and Income." Last updated December 2, 2020. https://www.ers.usda.gov/topics/farm-economy/farm-household-well-being/income-and-wealth-in-context/.

USDA ERS (United States Department of Agriculture Economic Research Service). 2021a. "Assets, Debt, Wealth." Last updated February 5, 2021. https://www.ers.usda.gov/topics/farm-economy/farm-sector-income-finances/assets-debt-and-wealth/.

USDA ERS (United States Department of Agriculture Economic Research Service). 2021b. "Farm Structure." Last updated January 6, 2021. https://www.ers.usda.gov/topics/farm-economy/farm-structure-and-organization/farm-structure/.

USDA ERS (United States Department of Agriculture Economic Research Service). 2021c. "Farming and Farm Income." Last updated February 5, 2021. https://www.ers.usda.gov/data-products/ag-and-food-statistics-charting-the-essentials/farming-and-farm-income/.

USDA ERS (United States Department of Agriculture Economic Research Service). 2021d. "Federal Government Direct Farm Program Payments, 2011-2020f Nominal (Current Dollars)." USDA ERS Data Product: Farm Wealth and Income Statistics. Last updated February 5, 2021. https://data.ers.usda.gov/reports.aspx?ID=17833.

USDA ERS (United States Department of Agriculture Economic Research Service). 2021e. "Soybean and Oil Crop; Related Data & Statistics." Last updated January 12, 2021. https://www.ers.usda.gov/topics/crops/soybeans-oil-crops/related-data-statistics/.

USDA FSA (United States Department of Agriculture Farm Service Agency). 2019. "Agriculture Risk Coverage (ARC) & Price Loss Coverage (PLC)." August 2019. https://www.fsa.usda.gov/Assets/USDA-FSA-Public/usdafiles/FactSheets/2019/arc-plc_overview_fact_sheet-aug_2019.pdf.

USDA GIPSA FGIS (United States Department of Agriculture Grain Inspection, Packers and Stockyards Act Federal Grain Inspection Service). 2014. "Subpart M – United States Standards for Wheat." In *U.S. Standards: May 2014*. Washington, DC: United States Department of Agriculture. https://www.gipsa.usda.gov/fgis/standards/810wheat.pdf.

USDA NASS (United States Department of Agriculture National Agricultural Statistics Service). 2017. "Appendix A, Census of Agriculture Methodology" in *2017 Census of Agriculture*. Washington, DC: United States Department of Agriculture. https://www.nass.usda.gov/Publications/AgCensus/2017/Full_Report/Volume_1,_Chapter_1_US/usappxa.pdf.

USDA NASS (United States Department of Agriculture National Agricultural Statistics Service). 2019a. *2017 Census of Agriculture: United States Summary and State Data*. Washington, DC: United States Department of Agriculture. https://www.nass.usda.gov/Publications/AgCensus/2017/Full_Report/Volume_1,_Chapter_1_US/usv1.pdf.

USDA NASS (United States Department of Agriculture National Agricultural Statistics Service). 2019b. *2017 Census of Agriculture Highlights: Farms and Farmland*. Report No. ACH17-3/August 2019. https://www.nass.usda.gov/Publications/Highlights/2019/2017Census_Farms_Farmland.pdf.

USDA NASS (United States Department of Agriculture National Agricultural Statistics Service). 2019c. "Census of Agriculture: Frequently Asked Questions." Last updated December 4, 2019. https://www.nass.usda.gov/AgCensus/FAQ/2017/index.php.

USDA NASS (United States Department of Agriculture National Agricultural Statistics Service). 2020a. *2017 Census of Agriculture Highlights: New and Beginning Producers*. ACH17-23, November 2020. Washington, DC: United States Department of Agriculture. https://www.nass.usda.gov/Publications/Highlights/2020/census-beginning%20-farmers.pdf.

USDA NASS (United States Department of Agriculture National Agricultural Statistics Service). 2020b. *Farm Labor*. ISSN: 1949-0909. Washington, DC: United States Department of Agriculture. https://downloads.usda.library.cornell.edu/usda-esmis/files/x920fw89s/n583zg017/dn39xm85z/fmlao520.pdf.

USDA NASS (United States Department of Agriculture National Agricultural Statistics Service). 2020c. *Farms and Land in Farms 2019 Summary*. Washington, DC: United States Department of Agriculture. https://www.nass.usda.gov/Publications/Todays_Reports/reports/fnloo220.pdf.

USDA NASS (United States Department of Agriculture National Agricultural Statistics Service). 2020d. *Land Values 2020 Summary (August 2020)*. Washington, DC: United States Department of Agriculture. https://www.nass.usda.gov/Publications/Todays_Reports/reports/lando820.pdf.

USDA NASS (United States Department of Agriculture National Agricultural Statistics Service). 2020e. *Milk Production*. ISSN: 1949-1557. Washington, DC: United States Department of Agriculture. https://downloads.usda.library.cornell.edu/usda-esmis/files/h989r321c/z603rf49q/b2774d05q/mkpro220.pdf.

USDA NRCS (United States Department of Agriculture Natural Resources Conservation Service). n.d. "Animal Feeding Operations." Accessed February 21, 2021. https://www.nrcs.usda.gov/wps/portal/nrcs/main/national/plantsanimals/livestock/afo/#:~:text=There%20are%20approximately%20450%2C000%20AFOs,for%20a%20large%20concentrated%20AFO.

US GAO (Government Accountability Office). 2018. *Working Children: Federal Injury Data and Compliance Strategies Could Be Strengthened.* GAO-19-26 (November). Washington, DC: US Government Accountability Office. https://www.gao.gov/assets/700/695209.pdf.

US SBA (United States Small Business Administration) Office of Advocacy. n.d. *2019 Small Business Profile.* Washington, DC: US Small Business Administration Office of Advocacy. https://cdn.advocacy.sba.gov/wp-content/uploads/2019/04/23142719/2019-Small-Business-Profiles-US.pdf.

Vaughn, Barrett, LeRosha Ford, Silvia Brashier, Miles Robinson. 2019. "H-2A Temporary Agricultural Workers on Small Farms: Case Study Observations and Lessons Learned." *Professional Agriculture Workers Journal* 7 (1) (October): 1-10. https://tus-pubs.tuskegee.edu/cgi/viewcontent.cgi?article=1124&context=pawj.

Vietmeyer, Noel. 2011. *Our Daily Bread: The Essential Norman Borlaug.* Lorton, VA: Bracing Books.

Wertz, Joe. 2020. "Farming's Growing Problem." *The Center for Public Integrity,* January 22, 2020. https://publicintegrity.org/environment/unintended-consequences-farming-fertilizer-climate-health-water-nitrogen/.

Western Growers. 2020. "Farmers: The Original Environmentalists." *Western Growers* (blog), March 23, 2020. https://www.wga.com/magazine/2020/03/23/farmers-original-environmentalists#:~:text=The%20fact%20is%3A%20Farmers%20are,the%20environment%20was%20a%20cause.

White House. 2019. "Remarks by President Trump at the American Farm Bureau Federation's 100th Annual Convention | New Orleans, LA." January 15, 2019. https://www.whitehouse. gov/briefings-statements/remarks-president-trump-american-farm-bureau-federations-100th-annual-convention-new-orleans-louisiana/.

White, Monica M. 2018. *Freedom Farmers: Agricultural Resistance and the Black Freedom Movement.* Chapel Hill, NC: The University of North Carolina Press.

White, Monica M. 2019. "'A pig and a garden': Fannie Lou Hamer and the Freedom Farms Cooperative," *Food and Foodways* 25 (1) (February): 20-39. https://doi.org/10.1080/07409710.201 7.1270647.

Whitt, Christine. 2020. "A Look at America's Family Farms," United States Department of Agriculture (blog), January 23, 2020. https://www.usda.gov/media/blog/2020/01/23/ look-americas-family-farms.

Widmar, David and Brent Gloy. 2015. *The Farm Financial Situation: Using Historic Insights to Evaluate Current Conditions.* A Report for the Farm Credit System Coordinating Committee (December 5, 2015). Westpoint, IN: Agricultural Economic Insights, LLC. https://www.farmcrediteast.com/-/media/ farm-credit-east/News/2016/Files/gloywidmar-the-farm-financial-situation-final.ashx?la=en.

Williamson, James M. 2013. "Agriculture, the Tax Code, and Potential Tax Reform" *Choices* 28 (2) (April): 1-5. http:// choicesmagazine.org/choices-magazine/theme-articles/

innovations-to-support-beginning-farmers-and-ranchers/
potential-challenges-for-beginning-farmers-and-ranchers.

WWOOF USA (World Wide Opportunities on Organic Farms
USA). n.d. "Home Page." Accessed February 21, 2021. https://
wwoofusa.org/.

Zinn, Howard. 1990. *A People's History of the United States.* New
York: Harper & Row.

Zulauf, Carl. 2020. "Age of US Farmers: Is the Wrong Issue Being
Addressed?" *farmdoc daily* 10 (35) (February): 1-2. https://farm-
docdaily.illinois.edu/2020/02/age-of-us-farmers-is-the-wrong-
issue-being-addressed.html.

Zulauf, Carl and Ben Brown. 2019. "Cover Crops, 2017 Census
of Agriculture," *farmdoc daily* 9 (135) (July): 1-3. https://farm-
docdaily.illinois.edu/2019/07/cover-crops-2017-us-census-of-
agriculture.html#:~:text=Cover%20crops%20in%20the%20
US,2.6%25%20in%202012.